FRANCE
from the AIR

France: your name is diversity
(F. Braudel, *L'Identité de la France*)

To Stefano Fantoni

WHITE STAR
PUBLISHERS

FRANCE *from the* AIR

Photographs
Guido Alberto Rossi

Text
Jean Louis Houdebine

Graphic design
Anna Galliani

Translation
David Stanton

North American edition
Managing editor JoAnn Padgett
Project editor Elizabeth McNulty

CONTENTS

1 Designed for Francis I by Leonardo da Vinci, the château de Chambord is one of the jewels of Renaissance architecture in the Loire valley.

2–3 The boundless landscapes of the north.... At Wissant, on the Côte d'Opale, between two curiously named promontories—the Blanc-Nez and the Gris-Nez (White Nose and Gray Nose)—at low tide the beach of fine sand reveals its colors with almost indefinable tones.

4–5 Another marvel of the Renaissance in the Loire valley: Chenonceaux and the peaceful beauty of its "French gardens" on the banks of the Cher.

6–7 Like huge ships riding at anchor in a port, the two islands around which the ancient Lutetia gradually developed on both sides of the river are in the center of this panoramic view of Paris: in the foreground is the Île de la Cité and the cathedral of Notre-Dame, further away lies the Île Saint-Louis.

ISBN 88-8095-362-1

Color separations Fotomec Turin
Graphic Service, Milan
Printed in Italy by Grafiche Mazzucchelli

8 Alsatian by nature, French by choice, Strasbourg is also the quintessence of the European city, the seat of the parliament of the fifteen countries of the European Union.

9 Dominating the majestic scenery of its immense bay, Mont-Saint-Michel bears witness to the religious and artistic splendor of the Middle Ages.

10–11 Soaring above the valley of Chamonix and a favorite with alpinists and skiers, the huge massif of Mont Blanc includes the highest mountain in Europe (4,807 meters or 15,771 feet).

Introduction

by JEAN LOUIS HOUDEBINE

Even for those of us who are accustomed to aerial photography, there is nothing more astounding than discovering from above (from a plane window, a helicopter cabin or simply the top floor of a modern tower block) the places that are most familiar to us—the town where we live, the streets we have gone along a thousand times, the landscapes we thought we knew in every detail. Nothing is more revealing: it is as if suddenly space were investing us with its real dimension, now imbued with even stranger novelty, because, at the same time, we suddenly find ourselves recognizing a detail with amazement: it's right there that I live; I've passed by there very often; that's where I went on holiday with my parents or, later on, with my children. Seen from above, our "down there" takes on a curious aspect and all the prestige of the out of the ordinary is conferred on it. A different adventure begins. These fields, these rivers, these woods in the shade of which thousands of invisible roads criss-cross one another, and also these villages and sprawling cities: so I had never seen them before. At least, not in all their extent, from a vantage point that allows me to have an overall view.

In this way, and for the first time with such clarity, the forms of a city appear: the layout of its network of streets and its buildings, its ancient fortifications, the suburbs spreading out untidily toward the surrounding countryside. The ever mysterious courses of rivers and streams are revealed as they find a way round obstacles or else open up a gap where this seems impossible. And then there are the vast areas of color making up the surface of a plain or an area furrowed by valleys: meadows, cultivated fields, heathland and fallow land, a chequer-board formed by the living hedgerows in the wooded areas; or, on the coast, the perfect squares of the salt-marshes, the murky ochre of the estuary of a river flowing into the ocean.

There is no doubt that this is the main cause for amazement: the space within which we habitually move is the height of a man and, conditioned by our daily routine, it is nearly always limited or closed. From above, our field of vision acquires depth and a whole host of new viewpoints that are even more varied and unexpected if we are flying—as in my case—in a light aircraft or helicopter and we are free to circle around a particular feature, see it from the most inaccessible angles and approach or distance ourselves from it as we wish in order to have an even more surprising overall view that can stimulate intense sensations of wonder. Because, all said and done, this is the essence of the aerial photograph: it is an invitation to travel through the space and time of this country, France, which millions of tourists choose to discover or to revisit every year.

13 For over 60 km south of Dijon some of the finest vineyards in France extend along the hillsides. The vines are cultivated on the last slopes of the limestone plateaux overlooking the Saône valley: formerly known as the Côte de Nuits and Côte de Beaune, significantly the area is now called the Côte d'Or.

14 The jagged peaks of the Aiguille du Midi form a fantastic pattern of spires towering above the valley of Chamonix. It is here, under almost 2,500 meters (8,200 feet) of rock, that the Mont Blanc tunnel passes: over 11 km (7 miles) in length, since 1965 it has formed a direct link between France and Italy. On the other side, the Val D'Aosta descends toward Turin.

Since this is a journey that will give us a bird's eye view, let us attempt, first of all, as if this were a first reconnaissance flight, to have an overview of the country we are going to see from above. An image that is commonly used to described it (perhaps a little ironically) is a geometrical figure: the hexagon. Besides being anything but inappropriate (we only have to look at a map of France to see the six sides of this figure), we cannot avoid associating it with a well-known trait of the French mentality: that of the Cartesian spirit, as it often described, characterized by order, method and unity. Although, as we cross this hexagon, we soon realize that it is formed by an incredible variety of different aspects that has always impressed visitors over the centuries, with numerous marked contrasts being evident: the variety of landscape, climate (from wet to dry, harsh to mild, from oceanic to continental) and types of land (from the warm to the cold ones, fertile and barren); differences in elevation, comprising a great variety of terrain, from the peaks of some of the highest mountains in Europe (the Alps and the Pyrenees) to plains and valleys large and small, including a mosaic of massifs of medium height, plateaux, hills and hillocks all over a country that is fairly vast, but not excessively so, so they form the modulations of the country's unity, its infinitely complex identity, which may even verge on the bizarre or the capricious. To all this should be added 3,200 kilometers (2,000 miles) of coast, it too extremely diversified, on three sides of the hexagon: the stormy, often misty shores on the North Sea and English Channel; the powerful waves and tides of the Atlantic, driven by the westerly winds, from Brittany to the Basque region; the Riviera and the enchanting resorts of the Mediterranean coast, from Menton to Collioure, where the vicinity of Italy and Spain is palpable.

15 top Rock faces ideal for climbing, vast glaciers and snowy peaks with rounded forms as far as the eye can see: the massif of Mont Blanc is the most famous section of the French Alps. In summer and winter alike thousands of tourists come to admire its magnificent landscapes.

15 bottom In 1890 Joseph Vallot had the refuge bearing his name built on a rocky slope preceding the Bosses ridge at a height of 4,309 meters (14,137 feet); the highest refuge in Europe, it is accessible to only the most expert alpinists.

16–17 *Along the whole range of the Pyrenees, in the foothills of the mountains, the landscape is very irregular, with intense colors: the route from the Atlantic coast, in fact, crosses the Basque region and Béarn to reach Bigorre, between Tarbes and Lourdes. There* *are many picturesque spots in the mountains in the background—the valleys of the Cauterets and the Gavarnie and all the names that every year are music to the ears of the fans of the Tour de France cycle race: Aubisque, Tourmalet, Aspin.*

That all this diversity does not prejudice the stability and harmony of the nation is something that will never cease to be cause for surprise. In this regard, the same thing applies to the history of France: depending on one's point of view, it may it may be equally legitimate to stress the internal divisions, the civil wars, the revolutions—the least one can say is that there has been no shortage of these in this country—or else underline the effects, equally undeniable, of the political unification undertaken over a long period (from the Middle Ages onward), thanks to the initiative of a strongly centralized state (originally a monarchy and then a republic). Only

17 top The Pyrenees extend for 400 km (250 miles) from the Atlantic to the Mediterranean, along the border with Spain. On the French side there are various peaks (the Vignemale and Le Pic Long, for instance) that are over 3,000 meters (9,850 feet) in height.

thirty years ago, commenting on the age-old tendency of the French to be disunited, General de Gaulle wondered, tongue-in-cheek, how it was possible to govern a country that boasted over 350 types of cheese! In other words, there are over 350 different regions or "pays," such as Pays d'Auge, Pays de Caux, Pays de Béarn or Pays Basque, each proud of its own traditions!

It is well known that two thousand years previously, during the Roman conquest, Julius Caesar had made a similar observation (more seriously and without any reference to cheese), at a time when what we now call France was a vast territory where there were numerous

17 bottom Since the nineteenth century, an observatory has been located on the summit of the Pic du Midi, an offshoot of the Pyrenees in the center of Bigorre; more recently, a television transmitter has been erected there.

internal boundaries and many different peoples coexisted, although they were often quarrelsome, each firmly attached to its own independence. And the name of this land was used both in the singular (Gaul) and in the plural (the Gauls): indeed, in the Roman period in Lyons there was an amphitheatre "of the three Gauls."

Yet, as long ago as the first century A.D., it was the exceptional cohesion of the area that the Greek geographer Strabo chose to underline in terms that, two thousand years later, have not lost their validity and can still serve to guide us on our aerial tour. What he says is essentially that it is a country blessed by the gods, where the disposition of the places is not the result of chance, but rather "a plan that is, after a fashion, logical," which, if one thinks about it, "bears witness to the action of providence." At the basis of this famous assertion, often quoted (leaving aside providence) by leading historians and geographers of the twentieth century (from Vidal de la Blanche to Fernand Braudel), there is the recognition of the complete harmony between the land, the seas that wash its coasts to the north, west and south and the rivers branching out over the whole surface linking together practically all the regions of the country.

This is a great deal of truth in this. The most concrete and vivid image of this unity paradoxically based on great diversity continues to be, in fact, that of the abundance of rivers and streams flowing here, there and everywhere through the French countryside, seeming to draw, as if they were on the palm of a hand, lifelines along which are located towns and villages, ancient monuments and industrial centers, rural landscapes created by centuries of hard work and wild ravines and other natural features formed by the erosion of the rock. It is no coincidence that the vast majority of the departments (the territorial and administrative districts introduced by the French Revolution) are named after the rivers that cross them. It is sufficient to make a list of them for us to picture the vast variety of landscapes that one comes across when travelling through the different regions of France: going up the Loire from Loire-Atlantique to Haute-Loire, passing through Marne-et-Loire, Indre-et-Loire, Loir-et-Cher and Loiret; going downstream, almost in a straight line from the Saône and the Doubs to the mouth of the Rhône, the Bouches-du-Rhône; without forgetting what a famous German poet called "die schöne Garonne" (beautiful Garonne), the fame of which is linked, once again, to that of its tributaries, the Tarn and the Lot, before reaching the Dordogne at Bec d'Ambès and forming an estuary (the Gironde) extending over seventy kilometers (forty-five miles) inland, the tidal activity of which may be observed above Bordeaux. In the same way, one could quote dozens of other geographical names deriving from rivers, which immediately evoke impressions linked to the landscapes characterizing them, the special properties of the water and light, depending on the seasons: the sandy slowness of the Loire in the summer, from Blois to the Atlantic, dotted with islets thickly covered with vegetation that the winter floods never manage to completely uproot; the roaring force of the Rhône on days when the Mistral is blowing and there splendid views between Vienne and Valence, around Condrieu and Tournon, where the hills are covered by terraced vineyards; and the peaceful, pastoral fascination of the smaller rivers of the western regions, the Thouet, the Vendée, or that of the two rivers Sèvre distinguished by charming feminine adjectives, the Niortaise and the Nantaise. The former sluggishly crosses one of the most curious regions of France, the marsh of the Marais Poitevin, significantly known as the "green Venice," while the murky waters of the Nantaise flow tranquilly toward Nantes, passing through a narrow valley dominated by the ruins of ancient fortresses, Clisson and Tiffauges, still haunted by the disquieting ghost of Gilles de Rais, later to become the Bluebeard of European folk tales.

The main protagonists of this adventure are, therefore, four great rivers, the Rhône, the Seine, the Loire and the Garonne, with their tributaries flowing down from the main mountain chains: the Alps, the Pyrenees and the Massif Central. They will guide us in our wanderings. They will be the leitmotiv of the various chapters of this book, where we may peacefully linger in the places that we come across. First of all we shall follow the north-south axis along the Rhône corridor that, since time immemorial, has linked the Mediterranean regions of the south to northern Europe. The natural prolongation of the Rhône valley, in fact, is formed by the valleys of the Saône and Doubs; skirting the Jura

18 Nestling in a bend of the Aveyron, on the border between Rouergue and Quercy, Najac is a picturesque village in a hilly region with splendid scenery: far from the madding crowd, it has many delights in store for the discerning tourist.

19 A quiet village street leading to the church square situated a little higher up on a hillside: the sun is shining, it is August in a rural area of central France.

20 top In terms of its surface area, the principality of Monaco is minute. The lack of space has been compensated for by building upward and systematically constructing embankments, which has allowed almost a quarter of the present area to be reclaimed from the sea.

20 bottom The remarkable prosperity of Monaco began at the end of the nineteenth century: palaces and sumptuous villas sprang up around Monte Carlo and its famous casino, making it the favorite holiday resort of the rich and the mighty from then onward.

and Vosges, they lead to the Rhine valley, which for 190 kilometers (118 miles) forms the border with Germany. All the rivers from this point onward are oriented northward and flow toward Belgium, the Netherlands and Germany after having crossed, as the Meuse does, the Ardennes with their deep gorges, "immense forests of shrubs" and drenching rain; or else, like the Sambre, Escault and Lys, further west, on the northern borders, which flow from the hills of Artois, feeding the numerous canals that have contributed to the prosperity of Flanders.

For the hundreds of thousands of tourists who arrive every year from the regions of the north (both of France and of Europe) this is the holiday route *par excellence*, the "sunshine highway" leading to the regions that are a byword for the endless summer. Once you've passed Lyons then Valence, everything seems to change: finally you've arrived! The air seems noticeably warmer, the sky more luminous, the first olive groves appear, together with the holm-oaks, the pomegranates, the Provençal farmhouses with flat roofs and vaulted porticos. Finally, down there is Marseilles and the deep blue sea the warm waters of which immediately make you want to have a bathe and laze away the sunny afternoons on the beach.

20-21 This panoramic view of Monaco highlights the exceptional beauty of the area, to which must be added the myth (with an incontrovertible basis of truth!) of a comfortable life in the Mediterranean sunshine amidst luxury villas and millionaires' yachts.

And from Toulon to the Italian border extends what is always known as "la Côte," as if there were no other "coasts" in France—the Côte d'Azur, in other words: Menton; the principality of Monaco and its rocky promontory where, over the last century, numerous luxury hotels, dream villas and princely residences have sprung up, together with its legendary casino, that of Monte Carlo, where you can win and lose everything in an evening; Beaulieu-sur-Mer, Villefranche-sur-Mer and their splendid bays separated by the headland of Saint-Jean-Cap-Ferrat, where lemon and orange trees grow; Nice and its Promenade des Anglais on the sea front and the old town with its typically Italian colors (Nice was only ceded to France in 1860) and shady narrow streets thronged with lively crowds until late evening; Cannes and its Croisette invaded every spring by the international movie stars on the occasion of the film festival, the first of its kind to be established; and then the seaside resorts of Juan-le-Pins, La Napoule, Saint-Tropez. All of them are world-famous, to the extent that they could be described as victims of their own success, so overcrowded are they in the summer. The magic of this area expresses itself in all its splendor from above, with the majestic scenery of the interior extending to the foothills of the southern Alps: wonderfully sculpted rocky coasts, with their numerous promontories and small bays,

washed by a sea of an intense, transparent blue that, as in a Fauvist painting, sets off the dark red porphyry of Estérel, and further away, beyond the Argens stream, the deep green of the pinewoods, the cork-oaks and the chestnut trees of the Massif des Maures.

Off the coast we encounter the Hyères islands, Porquerolles and Port-Cros, both designated as national parks thanks to their rich Mediterranean flora and fauna, and the Levant island, a naturist paradise. Even further out to sea, at a distance of about two hundred kilometers, is Corsica. The fact that it has been called the "Île de Beauté" speaks volumes about the marvels that await the visitor: the mountain slopes of the interior thickly covered with maquis (Mediterranean scrub), the narrow valleys with their steep sides leading to small villages clinging to the heights above where life still seems to be governed by the changing seasons, the sheer rocky coasts overlooking the warm, limpid sea, as at Bonifacio or in the Bay of Porto. Ajaccio, Bastia and Corte are the main towns of this island with its touchy pride, divided (if not torn) between loyalty to France, of which it has been part since the eighteenth century (Napoleon is its most famous son) and its demands for independence, which are at least partially the result of the new importance given to the island's age-old traditions and culture.

Our route back to mainland France takes us through Provence with its landscape full of contrasts (the writer Jean Giono observed that there was not one Provence, but many): the wild, arid areas of Haute-Provence, with fortified villages perching on almost inaccessible rocky outcrops; olive groves and fields of flowers, such as those around Grasse, the town of a thousand perfumes; rows of cypresses standing out against the bright sky. It is easy to understand why this area has long been favoured by painters: Matisse and Picasso lived here for a long time; the pictures of Arles painted by Van Gogh are among his greatest masterpieces; as far as Cézanne is concerned, it is in Aix-en-Provence, his birthplace, that he executed his most outstanding works, returning every day to his "model," as he used to call it, in other words Mont-Sainte-Victoire, which did not fail to inspire him until the very end. The historical capital of Provence, Aix is now an artistic city, renowned above all for its music festival, during which it is a delight to stroll through its little squares where fountains play.

22 In the foreground is the Trinquetaille bridge at Arles, on the Rhône, in the brilliant light of the Provençal summer. A little higher up is the amphitheatre where bullfights have replaced the combats between gladiators of Roman times. On the right, not far from the church of Saint-Trophime, are the remains of the theatre built in the reign of Augustus.

23 top On the edge of the Camargue, Arles is the very epitome of Provence: beautiful, sun-drenched and carefree.

Close by, but surprisingly different is Marseilles—restless, turbulent Marseilles, together with Lyons the second city of France, the largest port in the Mediterranean, forever facing the East and Africa. An old Greek colony founded by the Phocaeans long before it was conquered by the Romans, it is certainly the French city that has been cosmopolitan for the longest time and most consistently: Greeks, Italians, Armenians and North Africans have settled here in successive waves of immigration, forming one of the liveliest and most colorful communities in the Mediterranean, which—with its mixture of cultures that may, at times, be explosive—is always passionate and warm-hearted. In certain sense the city may be said to resemble its famous dish, the bouillabaisse, which, with its strong flavours, can only be enjoyed in its original version down at the old port, at the Estaque, or near the coves of the Goudes or Cassis.

As we go up the Rhône to Lyons, we fly over towns bearing witness to the Gallo-Roman civilization, many splendid monuments of which still exist. This is the case of Arles and Orange, where the ancient theatre (built under Augustus, with its excellent acoustics) houses the fascinating opera season every summer. Not far from the river is the imposing aqueduct of Pont du Gard and the amphitheatre of Nîmes (the best-preserved in the whole of the former Roman Empire), where the famous bull-fights are held, an opportunity to remember to influence of the other great culture of south-western Europe, that of Spain. The ferias of Nîmes are an outstanding example.

Starting from Avignon, the ancient papal city, famous

for its theatre festival established in 1947 by Jean Vilar, the valley alternates between wide expanses and points where it forms narrow gorges, as at Donzère-Mondragon, formerly a stretch dreaded by boatmen, both when ascending and when descending the river, and now the site of an important hydroelectric power station; the latter is one of the large industrial schemes that have profoundly changed the course of the river and the appearance of its banks. The "wild bull coming down from the Alps," as Michelet called the Rhône in the nineteenth century, has largely been tamed. In the same way, in addition to the vineyards that were first culti-vated at the time of the Roman Empire and, from

25 top In the upper part of the photograph is the Opéra of Lyons, and just below the Hôtel de Ville overlooking Place Des Terreaux, adorned with a splendid monumental fountain in which four leaping horses represent the rivers flowing toward the ocean.

25 bottom Dominating the center of Lyons, the church of Notre Dame stands on the hill of Fourvière, from where there is a magnificent view of the city. But some prefer the splendid Gothic architecture of the cathedral of Saint-Jean, a little lower down the hill.

24–25 On the tongue of land between the Soâne and the Rhône are concentrated some of the most famous business areas of Lyons, embellished with large squares, such as the one in the center of the photograph, Place Bellecour.

Châteauneuf-du-Pape to Côtes-du-Rhône and Côte-Rôtie (south of Vienne), produce strong wines of an intense red color, at times almost ruby, numerous magnificent orchards (peaches, pears, cherries) have been planted in recent years, providing a splendid display of blossom in the spring. Seen from above the spectacle is even more striking because it is framed by the steep mountains: still relatively distant to the east (although the first slopes of the Massif du Vercors, for example, lie only about twenty kilometers from Valence), to the west they rise sheer above the river and continue thus to beyond Lyons.

Lying at the confluence of the Rhône and the Saône, at the meeting-point of the routes between the countries of northern Europe, Germany, Italy and the regions of central France, the former capital of the Gauls has always had close links with the rest of Europe. The Lyons conurbation has a population of over 1,200,000, while the Rhône-Alpes region, of which it is the capital, is one of the leading industrial centers in France. With a long history behind it and flourishing thanks to its numerous activities—industrial, commercial, academic and scientific—the city has often had a pioneering role: Lyons was, in fact, the first French industrial city (in the field of silk

and textiles) and the uprisings of the silk-weavers of 1831 and 1834 were the first of the many workers' rebellions that have characterized the nation's political history; on the other hand, as is well known, it was in Lyons at the end of the nineteenth century that the Lumière brothers invented cinematography. But perhaps the special genius of this city lies in a careful balance between conservatism and modernism, tradition and innovation. Rather than seeking to flaunt its qualities, Lyons is a place where refinement, based on *savoir-faire* acquired in the course of time, is the order of the day. After all, just to mention a few examples of the Lyonnais cuisine—the reputation of which is undisputed—not everyone is able to make quenelles of pike or pullet with truffle (cut into thin slices, which are then inserted between the meat and the skin,

and served in its stock). In the summer months, after enjoying a splendid meal, there is nothing better than a stroll along the banks of the Saône and the Rhône, or through the narrow streets of the old city, on the historic hills of Fourvière and Crois-Rousse.

Leaving the Dombes and its huge bird sanctuary between the lakes behind to the east, we head north up the valley of the Saône. This leads us straight to Burgundy, at the edge of which we encounter the magnificent ruins of Cluny Abbey, which was extremely influential from the religious, intellectual and artistic points of view in the early Middle Ages. Cluny is but the first example on our route of Romanesque architecture, sublime examples of which are to be found in this region: Fontenay and its wonderfully simple minster, the perfect expression of the

26–27 *The magnificent vineyards of Burgundy extend 60 kilometers (37 miles) at the foot of green hills from Dijon to Santenay.*

27 top *Gevrey-Chambertin, Clos-Vougeot, Meursault, Volnay, Pommard, Nuits-Saint-Georges; on the Côte-d'Or, south of Dijon, each village has its own* cru, *the names of which, to the ears of connoisseurs, are promises of delights to come.*

27 bottom *Mostly owners of their vineyards, the wine-growers of Burgundy certainly have got nothing to complain about: the* clos *(farms) where they live and work, like the one seen here, have a sturdy, unpretentious charm.*

Cistercian ideal tirelessly championed by St Bernard; Vézelay and its huge basilica on the hilltop, one of the main halting places for pilgrims on their way to Santiago de Compostela in Spain; and a host of other more modest churches, some of them simple chapels, the stones of which, with their delicate yellow ochre, like a halftone, convey a timeless sense of peace. Oddly enough—and without wishing to in any way offend the spirit of abstinence and poverty dear to St Bernard, this golden brown color is also found in the famous white wines of Chablis, and also those of Meursault, with their matchless bouquet. As far as the reds are concerned, the Côte-d'Or, where the vineyards extend continuously from Santenay and Beaune to Nuits-Saint-Georges and Dijon, produces a range of outstanding wines. Beaune the magnificent, with its glazed multicolored tiles, and Dijon with its Palace of the Dukes and States of Burgundy, epitomize a thriving province that was once a kingdom whose possessions extended as far as Flanders.

On this route, which was that of the dreams of glory entertained by the princes with their epic names—Philip the Bold, John Fearless, Philip the Good and his golden fleece, Charles the Reckless—we soon reach Lorraine and Alsace, then the broad plains of the north extending to the sea. Until fairly recently these could be called perilous regions (that is, before the process of European unification): over the centuries—the Second World War was the last dramatic case in point—it is here that the invasions have begun. The history of France is full of names of battles (victories or defeats) that were fought in these places on the country's periphery: Azincourt, Rocroy, Valmy, Sedan, Verdun. At an early date the cities of Lille and Cambrai to the north and Metz and Toul to the east

became strongholds intended to prevent as far as possible the crossing of a border that was only too vulnerable. In the seventeenth century, under Louis XIV, Sébastien Le Prestre de Vauban was the military engineer who constructed these splendid fortifications with their masterly geometry comprising angle-bastions and demilunes; their polygonal plans continue to dominate the centers of such fortified towns as Le Quesnoy, Mézières and Neuf-Brisach, near Colmar.

Alsace is a magnificent region, and it is easy to understand why it has been so bitterly disputed over the last four centuries. Despite its very evident Germanic tradition, the region's loyalty to France, as often happens in border areas, has always been very strong, even before the 1789 revolution and the proclamation of the first republic: it is no coincidence that one of the most picturesque quarters of Strasbourg, not far from the splendid Gothic cathedral, is called "la petite France" (just as Colmar has its "little Venice"). This has not, however, prevented this city from becoming, together with Brussels and Luxembourg, one of the three capitals of modern Europe (it is the seat of the European parliament), and in this sense it is true to its name, "Strassen-burg"—in other words, "the city of the roads" that meet here. And the Kehl bridge, linking the two banks of the Rhine, is rightly considered to be an important symbol of Franco-German reconciliation.

At the foot of the eastern slopes of the Vosges, with their thick woods of beech and fir, there are numerous small towns that display their prosperity with peaceful splendor: in the enchanting half-timbered houses and their flower-decked balconies adorned with carvings, and even more in the vineyards that grow between Mutzig, Sélestat and Colmar, and also at Riquewihr, where one of Alsace's most renowned wines, Riesling, is produced. Alsace is indeed a land of milk and honey—it is said that when he saw it for the first time, Louis XIV exclaimed: "What a beautiful garden!"

Once we have headed west over Lorraine and passed the Meuse near Verdun, the main rivers we encounter flow toward the Seine: the Aube and the Marne, which cross Champagne south of Reims, the city where the cathedral is adorned with 2,300 figures on the façades, including the gallery of the kings in which, above the huge rose window, are ranged 56 statues, each 4.5 meters in height, reminding us that it was here that the king of France came to be crowned; and finally the Oise, which comes from Picardy, a huge muddy plain golden with corn in the summer, flowing into the Seine just north of Paris.

28 Between the Moselle and the canal linking the Marne to the Rhine, the octagonal plan of the fortifications of Toul, in Lorraine, appears very clearly, with the salient angles of its eight bastions, built by Vauban in the seventeenth century. Like Metz and Verdun, Toul was for a long time a strategic stronghold contested by the kingdom of France and the Germanic Holy Roman Empire.

29 The construction of Reims Cathedral, a masterpiece of Gothic architecture—the apse and a sequence of flying buttresses decorated with spires are visible here—lasted a century (1211–1311). The façade of this royal cathedral, where the kings of France came to be crowned, is adorned with superb statues.

Thus everything leads toward the Île-de-France where the political unity of the nation began, and the city that lies on a loop in the river, the metropolis *par excellence*. The view from the air allows us to clearly distinguish the concentric circles of the successive stages in the historical development of the city: in the center, around the Île de le Cité, the original site of the ancient Lutetia, extends medieval Paris—described by the poets Rutebeuf and François Villon—which the walls constructed at the end of the eleventh century were intended to protect from invasions. With its 190,000 inhabitants, Paris was then by far the largest city in Europe, and the travellers of the day referred to it as a fascinating yet disquieting "Babylon." These first walls were subsequently extended on various occasions until the nineteenth century, when Baron Haussmann laid out the wide boulevards of modern Paris, while Montmartre and Belleville, on their respective hills, have still largely maintained a village atmosphere. Lastly, on the edge of the city, appears the circle of the boulevards of the marshals (each of them bears the name of a marshal of the Napoleonic Empire), which, in the 1960s, was surrounded by the external ring-road (the Périphérique), reserved for motor traffic.

There is no better way to appreciate the beauty and historical complexity of this city than to take a stroll along the banks of the Seine, for example from the Pont de Austerlitz to the Eiffel Tour. Notre-Dame, the Île Saint Louis and its ancient private palaces, the Tour Saint Jacques, the Sainte-Chapelle and the Conciergerie, the Pont-Neuf of Henry IV, the Louvre (now one of the world's great museums), Les Tuileries, the Musée d'Orsay, the Place de la Concorde, the Trocadéro: it is rare to find so many monuments of a long and eventful

history packed into such a small area. It is just a few kilometers that one can easily cover on foot, lingering in front of the *bouquinistes* selling their books here and there, or simply admiring the view, the flow of the river-water, its light color slightly darkened by the stone, and the diffused luminosity of the air. This is the Paris of the kings and revolutions, the Bastille and the Étoile-Champs-Elysées, the Pigalle, Montmarte, Montparnasse and Saint-Germain-des-Prés: there is no place, no name that does not immediately call to mind a flood of collective memories, those that constitute the living memory of a people. Few cities have been so widely praised, recounted, painted and sung, in all possible ways, by the most outstanding poets and the humblest street artists. Theatres, cinemas, cabarets, jazz clubs, all manner of museums, bookshops and libraries, simple bistros and elegant restaurants: who can claim to have made a truly complete tour of Parisian life? At the center of a vast conurbation that now has over eleven million inhabitants, and where one must admit life is far from always being easy, especially in times of crisis as at present, the city continues to attract and enchant huge numbers of visitors.

Although the disasters of post-war urbanization have not spared the environs of Paris (especially to the north and east), the more distant suburbs have often maintained their picturesque character. Thus there are the woods of Chantilly, Rambouillet and Fontainebleau, the Chevreuse valley with its peaceful villages, together with a fantastic range of châteaux, sumptuous royal or princely residences, such as Sceaux, Vaux-le-Vicomte and its park in French style, a

30 It is impossible today to imagine Paris without the Eiffel Tower, a masterpiece of engineering symbolizing the modernity of the industrial age. The controversy aroused by its construction at the end of the 1880s has long been forgotten and every year it attracts huge numbers of visitors.

31 The Arc de Triomphe, in the center of Place de l'Étoile: twelve important boulevards converge on it, including the most famous of them all, the Champs-Élysées (positioned vertically in the upper part of the photograph) leading toward Place de la Concorde and the Tuileries Gardens.

masterpiece by André Le Nôtre. And obviously Versailles, where the gardens and the park of 17,000 hectares (42,000 acres) never fail to enchant visitors. But one may also be attracted by the rural atmosphere of the banks of the Seine: upriver from Paris, near Melun and Samois, the river is serenely elegant. The painter Alfred Sisley and the poet Stéphane Mallarmé lived the last years of their lives in this area, the former at Moret-sur-Loing, the latter at Valvins. Downriver, from Argenteuil or Chatou to the terraces of Saint-Germain-en-Laye and then on to Rouen and the sea, it is necessary to mention nearly all the Impressionist painters—for instance, Seurat, Renoir, Monet and Degas—who have immortalized the landscapes of the Île-de-France. How can one resist lingering for a while at Giverny, where Monet lived and worked from 1883 to 1926? The "red and green" house, the Japanese garden, the water-lily pond—"a flowerbed of water," as Marcel Proust described it—are still there, just as they are depicted in the famous paintings that have immortalized them. Beyond Giverny and Vernon, as we gradually enter the prosperous region of Normandy, the Seine seems to multiply its meanders at will: soon, in a dominant position on the river, we encounter the imposing ruins of Château-Gaillard, the fortress built at the end of the twelfth century by Richard Lionheart; then Rouen, an important modern industrial city where the historic center—which has three masterpieces of Gothic architecture, the cathedral of Notre-Dame and the churches of Saint Maclou and Saint Ouen—was very carefully restored after the Second World War. On the banks of the river between Rouen and Le Havre are situated the *pays* of Haute-Normandie: to the north, lies the Pays de Caux, with its vast fertile lands crossed by just a few narrow valleys, its half-timbered farmhouses surrounded by orchards and gentle slopes covered with beechwoods; this area ends abruptly with sheer cliffs overlooking the sea, characterized by strange forms created by the incessant erosion of the wind and tide, as at Étretat.

To the south is the Pays d'Auge and its Côte Fleurie, where such famous seaside towns as Deauville, Trouville

and Cabourg were the favorite holiday resorts of the Parisian society of the belle époque. Inland interminable stretches of meadowland alternate with small woods and orchards of cider apples. One of the leading stockbreeding areas of France, Normandy is a major producer of milk and the cheese that has become its symbol, Camembert, named after the village near Vimoutiers where it was first made two hundred years ago. It hardly needs to be stressed that in this region there is a special

32–33 *A splendid aerial view of Versailles. Thanks to the balance and diversity of the forms, the precision of the composition of the natural spaces and the monumentality of the perspectives, the classical aesthetic asserts itself here in a superb manner. In the lower foreground is the fountain of Apollo, the god symbolizing the Sun King. Proceeding upward, there is the Allée Royale; the fountain of Leto, the mother of Apollo and Artemis; the two parterres of water; and, finally, the imposing façade (680 meters or 2,231 feet in length) of the royal palace overlooking the park.*

passion for cuisine and the food here is first-rate. This is demonstrated by another local tradition, the *trou normand* (the "Normandy hole"), which consists in drinking, halfway through a meal, a glass of calvados (apple brandy distilled from cider), which serves to give diners a fresh appetite so they can start from the beginning again. It's all been carefully worked out.

After the hills of Normandy, south of the long peninsula of Cotentin, the wonder of wonders, Mont-Saint-Michel, appears on its granite islet surrounded by immense banks of quicksands that the sea submerges completely at high tide. The spectacular bay, in which the elegant lines of the Benedictine abbey stand out

31 *On the Channel coast, near Fécamp, the erosion of the sea incessantly molds and transforms the strange shapes of the rocks.*

35 top *The vast fertile lands of the Pays de Caux, in Haute-Normandie, end brusquely with sheer chalk cliffs towering above the sea.*

35 center *At the mouth of the Rance, facing Saint-Malo, the resort of Dinard has long been a favorite with British and American tourists.*

35 bottom *Fishermen (called "Terre-Nuevas") who fished cod across the Atlantic near Newfoundland ("Terre-Neuve" in French), set sail from the port of Fécamp.*

against the sky, traditionally marks the border between Normandy and Brittany. However, Brittany is divided into a coastal region (Armorica, the "the land of the sea") and an inland one (Argoat, "the land of the woods"), and then there is the area of the Breton language (to the west of an imaginary line linking Guingamp to Vannes) and a Gaulish land (both French and Breton were spoken)—once again there are a thousand contradictions! The coast itself is a world apart: 1,200 kilometers (746 miles) of coastline that without the innumerable inlets and headlands would only be some 600 kilometers (373 miles) in length. Their indented forms contain marked contrasts: there are beaches of fine sand (for instance, at La Baule or Sables-d'Or-les-Pins), high sandstone or granite cliffs, such as those at Cap Fréhel or Pointe du Raz, against which the waves break incessantly, and, just about everywhere, rocky slopes in which, at intervals, small picturesque bays open onto the surging sea, where the air is charged with iodine. In some places deep fjords have been formed by the mouths of the rivers, as in the case of the superb panorama of Dinan, Dinard and Saint Malo, or there are vast estuaries, such as the *abers* in Finesterre, which extend inland for a considerable distance; or else there are wide inlets, such as that of Morbihan, forming a small inland sea (which is what its name means) studded with dozens of tiny islands. And then there are numerous harbours, both marinas for pleasure boats and commercial ports: Douarnenez, Concarneau and its "closed city" behind granite ramparts, Saint Malo with its fascinating history of pirates and adventurous navigators (Jacques Cartier, the explorer of Canada, Surcouf, Chateaubriand, the first great romantic writer), Roscoff, from where one may take a boat to the nearby island of Batz, as well as England and Ireland. And obviously there is Brest, which, after being completely destroyed during the last war, was rebuilt and became once again the leading French naval port, the deep-water harbour of which can contain ships of considerable tonnage. Lastly, off the coast, all the way to Nantes, there are large numbers of islands, including the most important, rightly called Belle-Île. Forty-five minutes by ferry from the mainland, this epitomizes many of the features of Brittany: the sheltered beach on the east coast, the rugged interior, with coombs and rock faces, in which ravines and caves have been eroded, cliffs swept by wind and waves, and, to

*36 top The name of Belle-
Île, off the coast of Brittany,
speaks for itself: the sheer
cliffs of the Côte Sauvage,
pounded by the waves; the
beaches sheltered from the
wind on the east coast;
rocky coves concealing
small harbors; narrow
valleys leading inland to
moorland bright with gorse
and lush meadows—the
many-sided beauty of Belle-
Île never ceases to amaze
and delight the visitor.*

the west, the Côte Sauvage, beyond which lie only the vast
expanses of the Atlantic.

More secret, and certainly less well known, inland Brittany has its own appeal too, which makes it one of
France's most fascinating regions. Its attractions range
from the austere landscape of the Arrée hills, gorse-cov-
ered moorland and age-old forests such as that of
Paimpont, the medieval Brocéliande (unfortunately, even
Merlin and Vivian could not prevent being this being dev-
astated by a particularly violent storm about ten years ago)
to ancient fortresses with grim granite walls, such as those
at Vitré, Fougères and Josselin, and the modest mansions
of the lesser nobility that, in Brittany, never managed to
become particularly wealthy. Here and there in the countryside, from behind a hilltop or a hedge appear those
astonishing prehistoric monuments known as dolmens and
menhirs, of which the famous alignments at Carnac form
what is still today one of the most mysterious groupings.
What exactly was their function? They seem to be per-

vaded with the contemplative spirit that is echoed by the
region's churchyards of the sixteenth and seventeenth
centuries, where there is a solemn atmosphere, a little
lugubrious even, with special attention being paid to the
dead disposed about the church, which always has a Way
of the Cross and an ossuary.

Heading southward now, we encounter very different
regions, with milder, less rugged landscapes. In effect, they
begin with the Loire, the longest river in France (1,020 kilometers or 634 miles in length), which crosses the area from
east to west for practically the whole of its width and thus
forms the main dividing line between north and south, as
may be seen practically every evening in the weather fore-
casts on television. South of the Loire, from Poitou and
Limousin onward, they even used to speak a different lan-

36 bottom Situated on the southern edge of Brittany at the mouth of the Bay of Grand Traict, Le Croisic is not only a popular seaside resort but also a busy fishing port, with oyster beds occupying a large part of the bay.

36–37 The Vauban Citadel dominates the harbor of le Palais, the most important on Belle-Île: it is here that the tourists arriving from Quiberon land after a forty-five-minute crossing.

guage: this was the land of the *langue d'oc*, in contrast to the *langue d'oïl* (the two ways of saying yes in medieval French) that was spoken north of the river. What remains today is the singsong accent of the French spoken in the south, which, however, varies considerably: the accent of Marseilles or Toulon is very different from that of Narbonne and the eastern Pyrenees, which is almost a hoarse mumble, just as the accent of Nîmes has little in common with that of Toulouse or Bordeaux.

Situated on this dividing line between north and south, the landscapes of the Loire valley are, in reality, in a sort of delicate balance, which is all the more remarkable if one considers that the river flowing through them has always been known for its sudden changes of mood and its considerable seasonal variations. Unlike the Rhône, the Loire has not been tamed and is one of the few European rivers still in its natural state. But those living along its course are quite accustomed to its caprices, and then it is so beautiful in the summer. In the area round Mauves and Montsoreau the countryside has an infinity of nuances that match perfectly the delicate colors of the slate and tufa with which the houses between Tours and Angers are traditionally built, while the grapes ripening along its banks or on the surrounding hills at Champigny, Bourgueil and Chinon, produce wines that are smooth to the palette. Light wines, with a bouquet of violets or raspberries, their strength may vary from year to year: there are the good years and others that are less so, but, as I have already said, the Loire is like that, always unpredictable. The whole region seems to tend toward a sort of light-hearted joy, the art of living in harmony with bountiful nature that only seeks to collaborate with the works of man. "The garden of France" was how Rablais described the area; he was a native of Chinon, the favorite holiday town of the kings of France during the Renaissance. The court enriched the valley with its sumptuous residences: especially Chambord and Chenonceaux. Other famous châteaux are located at Sully-sur-Loire, Blois,

Azay-le-Rideau and Amboise, where Leonardo da Vinci stayed in 1516, before ending his days peacefully nearby, in the château of Cloux. These places form part of the famous tour of the Loire valley, which, every year, attracts thousands of visitors from all over the world.

It is in this stretch of the valley that the most magnificent châteaux are to be found. The imposing fortress that towers above the Maine in Angers is altogether another matter: the symbol of the short-lived power of the Angevin kings, who also reigned over Provence and the Kingdom of Naples and Sicily, it is also a reminder the past, of the brutality that in reality was fairly widespread, as is also attested by the fortified castles of Langeais (one of the keeps dates back to the tenth century), Luynes (twelfth century) and even more that of Loches, with its sinister Martelet where Louis XI kept important prisoners in cages made of iron and wood that he called, with what was decidedly macabre humor, "my little girls." Yet it's all so fascinating.... And the castles that one encounters further south, as one advances into the more inaccessible, desolate area of the Massif Central, have also largely maintained their aspect of medieval fortresses. They were built in places chosen essentially for the strategic position offering purely military advantages, but obviously it is the uncommon beauty of their ruins that attracts us today, and this is often given greater prominence by the notable isolation of the sites and the breathtaking contours of the hills. Thus the remains of the castle of Crozant stand on a rocky spur in the valley of the Creuse, guarding the access to Limousin. In the woods to the east of Tulle lies the château de Ventadour, which, thanks to its extraordinarily deep moats, could only be taken by treachery. And again, clinging to a crag the walls of which are surrounded by the Maronne, are the Tours de Merle, unconquered until the artillery stepped in, and there are dozens of other historical sites of a similar kind.

38 and 39 With its tall towers, the château d'Ussé, on the banks of the Indre in Touraine, overlooks splendid gardens and terraces. It is said that Charles Perrault, the author of universally

known fairy tales, was inspired by this castle to write the Sleeping Beauty, *in which the heroine waits for Prince Charming to come and free her from the spell of the fairy Carabosse.*

To tell the truth, it would take many pages to describe the magnificent landscape of these central regions, which stretch as far as the Cévennes to the south and extend from Périgord in the west, with hundreds of castles and its refined cuisine based on truffles, foie gras and comfits, to beyond the chain of extinct volcanoes of the Auvergne, around Clermont-Ferrand. A flight over these areas clearly reveals their contrasts, the result of their uneven terrain where there are series of rocky elevations that are either rugged or rounded and covered with pasture-land; volcanic lakes with their still, perfectly pure water, the woods of chestnut and holm-oak in Périgord; the plateau of Limousin with its vast areas of grassland; the narrow valleys of the Dordogne and Lozère, the steep sides of which, with their caves, provided shelter for prehistoric men, such as the Cro-Magnon cave at Les Eyzies-de-Tayac, where a huge quantity of invaluable archaeological and artistic remains have been discovered, as at Lascaux; the limestone plateaux and gorges of the Causses, with their harsh interminable winters, underground rivers and deep chasms that, in the last hundred years have made this area a favorite with speleologists; the arid, boundless solitude of

the Cévennes, the largest national park in France, covering the area extending from Mont Lozère to Mont Aigoual, where it is still possible to see golden eagles gliding high above. This area has a long-standing tradition of resistance, like Languedoc, which lies to the south of it; it is a land of opposition to the hegemony of the north, the usurper of power. Thus there was the resistance of the Cathars in the thirteenth century, then the resistance of the Protestants: at the end of the seventeenth century the Cévennes became the "desert" of the Camisards who were struggling against religious persecution and they were the scene of the atrocities committed on the occasion of the infamous dragonnades; and, during the Second World War, Mont Aigoual was one of the most important centers of resistance to the Nazi occupation.

Generally speaking, in these isolated areas, far from the main modern communication routes, one comes across such a variety of landscapes of exceptional natural beauty or of great historical interest—but frequently little-known—that one has the impression, perhaps more than elsewhere in France, of not being able to exhaust their features of interest and that something always remains to be discovered.

We shall now conclude our wanderings by allowing ourselves to be conveyed southwestward, where the "belle Garonne" awaits us. It is sufficient to follow the rivers that join it as it flows toward the Atlantic: the Tarn, the Lot and the Dordogne. Aquitaine is the traditional name of this region (the Romans called it Aquitania), which extends from the Pyrenees to Saintonge. It is also known as the "land of the waters" and, in fact, they certainly are not lacking: here we are in a totally different Midi, with the beneficial spring rains and numerous watercourses. The *gaves* rush down from the mountains and flow through Bigorre, Béarn and the vineyards of Jurançonnais to the Basque region with its intensely green hills that seem to make the white stucco of the houses even brighter; there is also the wide curve the Adour forms across Gascony, before it, too, flows into the Atlantic at Bayonne; then we reach the vast lakes of the Landes linked together by streams that flow through the immense forest of maritime pines, separated from the Atlantic by high dunes extending for 230 kilometers (143

40 bottom For centuries vineyards have been an integral part of the landscapes of the south of France: this is the area near Carcassonne, and the blanquette of Limoux is a sparkling wine much appreciated by connoisseurs.

40–41 A solitary tractor, apparently lost amidst the furrows that it is making, and a deserted country road, without the shade of a single tree. It's summer, near Carcassonne, between the Aude and the Garonne, a land of vast, sun-drenched landscapes.

miles); and then, obviously, the huge valley of the Garonne as it flows north through Toulouse and Agen, or that of the Lot, an area particular noted for its market gardens.

The history of this region has been, in any case, very eventful; still today there are the "refuge villages" or *châteauforts*, where the population sought the protection of the Church or the feudal lord and his soldiers. Subsequently, for three centuries, Guienne and Gascony became English possessions: this was the period in which the fortifications were built up, and new towns and villages created on geometric plans forming a chequer-board pattern in which it is easy to observe the rectilinear layout, such as at Mirande or Marciac, which in the summer is now the venue of an interesting jazz festival. The local traditions are still very strong here, rooted as they are in a past that has practically turned each *pays* into a separate cultural entity. Obviously, this is equally true for the Basque region—even more so if one considers that it is the con-

tinuation of the Basque country on the other side of the Spanish border (there is a similar situation, albeit on a smaller scale, in French Catalonia, in the eastern part of the Pyrenees); but Bigorre, Béarn and Gascony have also kept their own identity that the modern world has not managed to completely eliminate. Basque pelota, the Landaise race, the famous bullfights of Bayonne and Dax, and even rugby, a sport of British origin that has caught on in all the regions of south-west France, are obvious examples. However, apart from these traits of deep-rooted regionalism, it is probably in the area around Bordeaux that the character of Aquitaine reveals itself in all its splendor: as the river proceeds toward the capital of the former province of Guienne, the valley widens and the presence of the Atlantic is increasingly felt. A gently bracing breeze blows in off the ocean along the sunny banks of the Gironde to the low hills of the Dordogne near to Libourne, contributing to

43 bottom Between the beach of Port-Vieux and that of the Basques, a meeting-place for surfers, this splendid villa is a typical example of the luxurious residences that have made Biarritz famous.

42–43 Biarritz in all its splendor, on the Basque coast, about twenty kilometers (12 miles) from the Spanish border. It was during the Second Empire that the small village where the inhabitants of Bayonne came to bathe on the backs of donkeys or mules was transformed into the fashionable resort that it still is today. Bottom left: the famous Rocher de la Vierge.

43 top Near Pointe Saint-Martin lighthouse is the Chambre d'Amour, a cave where two legendary lovers trapped by the high tide met their deaths.

the slow ripening of grapes that produce matchless wines, with character and distinction, the names of which are, to a connoisseur's ears, promises of delights to come: Pomerol, Saint-Émilion, Graves, Sauternes, Médoc.... To be perfectly frank, if there's one area of France where I would like to land at the end of this aerial tour, where I would want to stay for a long time, going from one château to the next for interminable tasting sessions, then this is it! After all, was it not from the heights of the Pyrenees that, while returning from their Spanish forays and seeing Aquitaine's pleasant land stretching out before their eyes that the uncouth warriors in the *Chanson de Roland* (eleventh century) suddenly realized that they were at last back in "douce France"? This expression may seem paradoxical in view of the fact that this is an epic poem about which the least one can say is that it is characterized—like history as a whole— more by "shouting and fury" than "sweetness." Yet in a way this term sounds right: its truth is due first and foremost to the specific qualities of the majority of French landscapes, their contrasts that always end up by balancing each other, their infinitely varied, soft tones that the Impressionist painters were able to render in a particularly fascinating manner. And even more it is, no doubt, due to the *douceur* of life here, the refined nature of the lifestyle the taste for which—others, less optimistically, would say the dream, the chimera—has remained very much alive in France, going against the tide with regard to the excesses and coarse simplifications imposed on us all too often by the demands of modern life.

Naturally, there's still a great deal we haven't seen, so we'll certainly have to come back! On the other hand, the Canal du Midi is not far away: it links Toulouse to Sète and the Mediterranean Sea of dear old Strabo. But we can also head north, following the Atlantic coast to the picturesque port of La Rochelle.... Nothing is preventing us from leaving again. It's up to you!

44–45 A landscape crossed by shallow valleys, fields with marvellously irregular outlines, crops of all shades of ochre and green—from the lightest to the darkest—the intersection of two roads, one with capricious curves, the other impeccably straight: this aerial view is a spectacular epitome of the French countryside.

MOUNTAIN TREASURES

46 When flying over Mont Blanc it is possible to catch a glimpse here and there, between the enormous masses of rock covered with snow, of the valley of Chamonix. It is easy to understand why the position of this resort, at the foot of the highest peaks of the massif, has made it the capital of alpinism: among those fond of the mountains, it is renowned for its association of Alpine guides, founded in 1823.

47 The Mont Blanc Massif is situated on the border between France and Italy. The Italian side, shown here, is much steeper than the French one, and it is necessary to be an expert rock-climber to tackle it, a skill possessed by only a few accomplished alpinists. This aerial view of Mont Blanc highlights the size of the rock masses with their rough surfaces that are only partially mantled by the immense expanses of snow.

48 top *Winter sports are now very popular and many Alpine villages have been transformed into resorts able to accommodate thousands of skiers. This photograph shows Méribel.*

48–49 Extremely pleasant in summer too, Chamonix is very popular with hikers at this time of year. But it is also possible to ski at the Vallée Blanche, which can be reached by the Aiguille du Midi cableway.

49 top The splendid position of Chamonix, at the foot of the famous aiguilles, the sharply pointed peaks soaring almost 3,000 meters (9,800 feet) above the valley.

49 bottom In the summer, the Alpine valleys, in the bottom of which small villages nestle with their houses built to withstand the rigors of the harshest winters, offer innumerable opportunities for hiking or even just relaxing strolls.

50–51 The sublime spectacle of the high mountains. City-dwellers cannot help being fascinated by the huge dimensions of a landscape that inevitably appears to be out of scale with their usual surroundings. But woe betide those who think they can venture forth without adequate preparation: this no place for improvisers!

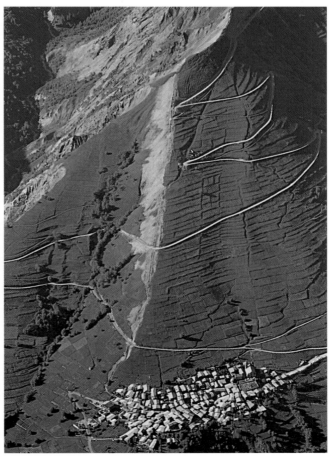

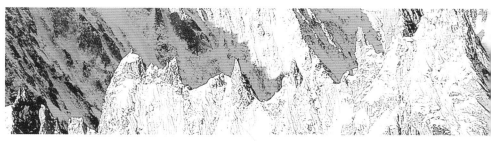

52 The pyramidal form of the Aiguille Verte (north face), the name of which derives from the greenish color of its granite rocks.

53 top With its altitude of 4,807 meters (15,771 feet), Mont Blanc is the highest peak in Europe and it is easy to understand why the first ascent of the mountain, made in 1786 by Dr Michel Paccard and Jacques Balmat, a guide from Chamonix, was regarded as a heroic feat.

53 center On the left, Le Grand Capucin, one of the most famous peaks of the Mont Blanc du Tacul, to the east of the Mont Massif Blanc itself and Mont Maudit.

53 right center The Aiguille du Midi can be reached by cable-car: from the upper station there is a remarkable panoramic view over the valley of Chamonix, almost 3,000 meters (9,840 feet) below.

53 bottom A modest wooden cabin covered with sheet metal, which here seems to be balanced precariously on a rocky crag, the Vallot refuge is famous throughout the Mont Blanc area and has saved the lives of many alpinists caught in bad weather.

54–55 Sunset over the Mont Blanc Massif.

56-57 The marvelous tapestry of fields and meadows, dotted here and there with pretty villages in the Pays de Pigorre, near Lourdes.

57 top Although not as high as the Alps, the Pyrenees form an impressive barrier. On the other side, beyond the clouds, is Spain, and for the pilgrims on their way to Santiago de Compostela the crossing of the mountains through the Roncesvalles Pass was a terrible ordeal.

56 bottom and 57 bottom The peaks of the massif of Canigou, in the eastern Pyrenees, reach a maximum height of 2,784 meters (9,134 feet). Climbed for the first time in the eighteenth century, it is the best-known—and perhaps the most loved—mountain in the Pyrenees. Every summer in June, from the night of the 22nd until the dawn of the 24th, the Catalans living in this part of Roussillon and over the *border in Spain, in Catalonia, enthusiastically celebrate the feast of St. John the Baptist, the leading protagonist of which has for centuries been the peak of the Canigou. From the top of the massif, there are splendid views as far the Mediterranean coast; it is said that at certain times of the year it is possible to distinguish the heights above Marseilles, 250 kilometers (155 miles) away as the crow flies.* *58-59. The foothills of the Pyrenees are particularly uneven, with steep slopes overlooking deep ravines. Until recently, in the more accessible areas, it was normal practice to take the animals to graze on the high pastures in summer.*

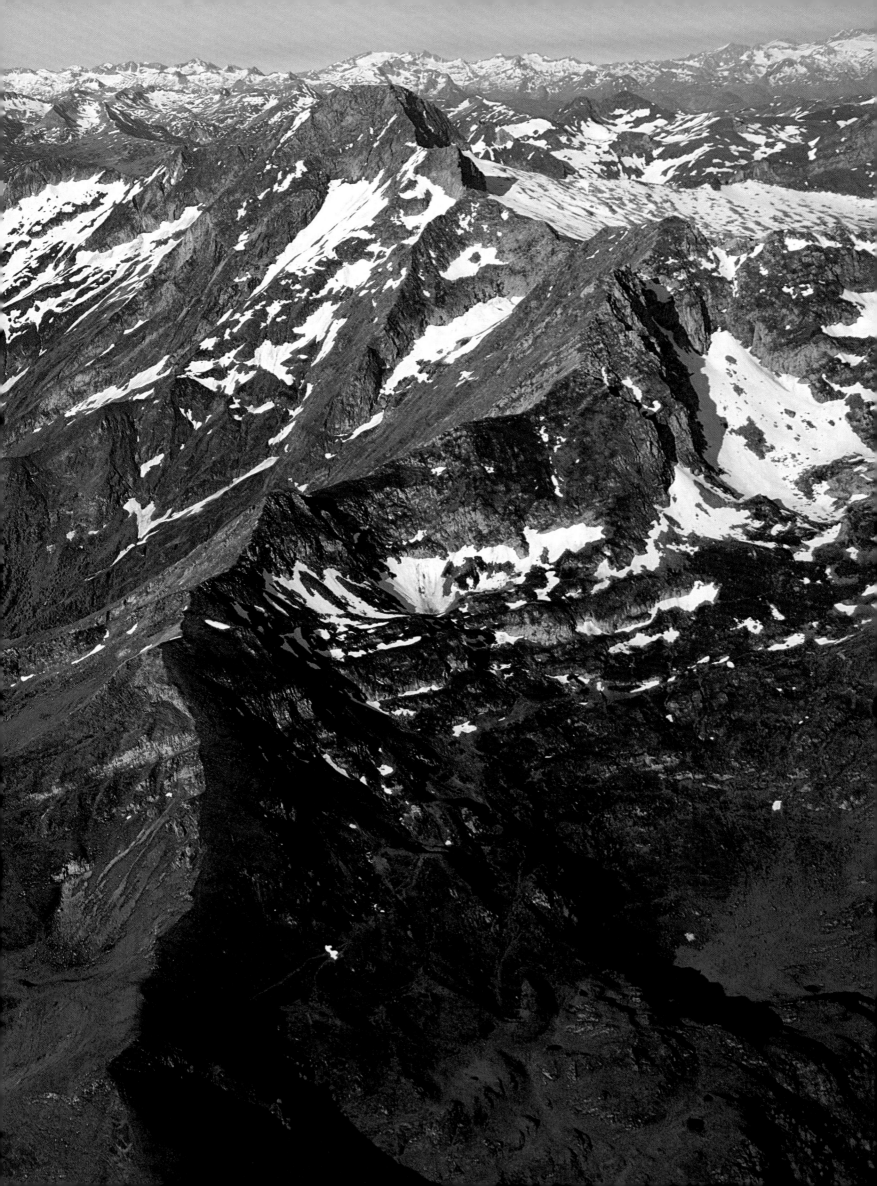

*60 top There are numerous
mountain lakes on the
French side of the Pyrenees
(over five hundred), adding
the fascination—always a
little mysterious—of their
silent waters to the verdant
splendor of the landscapes.*

*60–61 Often isolated from
each other at the bottom of
the Pyrenean valleys, small
villages grew up with their
traditional lifestyles that, in
may cases, have survived
until the present today.*

*61 bottom This row of wind
turbines installed on the crest
of the Pyrenees is one of the
new sources of energy that it
is hoped—with some
reservations, perhaps—will
have an important role to
play in the future.*

VILLAGES AND COUNTRYSIDE: A RURAL LIFESTYLE

62 Cap Gris-Nez, between Calais and Boulogne-sur-Mer marks the western boundary of Boulonnais–this point is only 32 kilometers (20 miles) from the English coast, which is visible on a clear day. With its vast flat expanses, the countryside is mainly devoted to the cultivation of cereals and beets. A little further south, for instance in the valley of Wimereux, stockbreeding is practised: formerly cart-horses, known as boulonnais were reared here.

63 The picturesque village of Najac, on the banks of the Aveyron, on a sleepy summer's day. With their own very special appeal, country holidays have become increasingly popular in France in the last few years.

64 top *West of the Cantal Mountains, in the Massif Central, at 950 meters (3,117 feet) above sea level, the small village of Salers has conserved intact—a heritage of its glorious past—the walls and towers that its citizens built in the* fifteenth and sixteenth centuries. *All the surrounding area, between Aurillac and Saint-Flour, is delightful and produces an excellent cheese—called cantal, naturally—that may be* jeune *(fresh),* vieux *(mature) or entre-deux (medium).*

65 bottom *On the Route des vins, in Alsace, from Marlenheim (north of Colmar) to Thann (to the south), vineyards are interspersed with villages, one more picturesque than the other, with their flower-decked balconies. It's a real land of milk and honey....*

64–65 and 66–67 *From Montbéliard to Besançon, at the foot of the first offshoots of the Jura, the River Doubs forms innumerable meanders round villages with churches having towers with Imperial domes (with four faces), typical of this region. The river's name is itself revealing: Doubs comes from the Latin* dubius, *meaning "undecided," "hesitant." At first flowing northwest, the river doubles back on itself through a gap in the Jura mountains; never ceasing to change direction, it flows for over 400 kilometers (249 miles) before reaching the Saône, although, as the crow flies, its source is only 90 kilometers (56 miles) away from its confluence.*

68 top In the upper part of the photograph, is visible the Rocher de Dabo, a sandstone spur the name of which derives from the powerful Dabo family, who ruled the region in the Middle Ages. An important member of this family was Leo IX, an eleventh-century pope who subsequently became St Leo, to whom the chapel on top of the rock is dedicated.

68 bottom The Pays de Dabo-Wangenbourg, south of Saverne, on the border between Alsace and Lorraine, is a region that is particularly rich in tourist attractions: medieval castles and huge woods with mountains rising on the horizon make it the ideal area for delightful long walks.

69 At over 700 meters (2,300 feet) above sea level, amid the woods surrounding the Route des vins, from Colmar to Saverne, the castle of Haut Koenigsbourg has stood since the twelfth century with its imposing forms. These have become even more impressive since the complex restoration work at the beginning of the twentieth century that Emperor William II commissioned a Berlin architect to carry out in the period (1871–1918), when Alsace and a portion of Lorraine formed part of Germany.

70 Surrounded by moats over ten meters (33 feet) in depth, the castle of Montmort-Lucy has, to a notable extent, maintained its feudal atmosphere. Like the nearby castle of Montmirail, it is, above all, associated with the great battle that took place at the beginning of the First World War, that of the Marne. It was here the general von Bülow announced that the advance of the German army had been halted and that it was time to begin the retreat.

71 top Amid the vineyards of the famous Côte des Blancs, in Champagne, the château d'Étoges is a splendid seventeenth-century residence surrounded by a moat full of water crossed by a picturesque bridge leading directly to the large courtyard.

71 bottom The small castle with four corner pepper-pot towers in the center of the photograph is what remains of the imposing fortress that the seigneurs of Dampierre built in the Middle Ages. It now forms the gateway to the château seen in the foreground: the latter, built in seventeenth century, reflects the classical mode, like the park in French style surrounding it.

72 On the Atlantic coast from Pointe de Grave to Hossegor there are interminable beaches and sandbanks on which the enormous Atlantic rollers break, to the great joy of surfers. In the interior, huge areas are covered by the maritime pines of the forest of the Landes, with their ample shade and sweet, heady perfumes.

73 The strange ochre color of the Gironde, the vast estuary of the Garonne, extending 75 kilometers (47 miles) from Bordeaux to the Atlantic. Fish is caught with nets suspended from the banks or from small boats, as seen here, or else from the top of the platforms built on the chalk rocks of the coast between Meschers and Royan.

74 top The Bec d'Ambès is located at the point where the Garonne and the Dordogne converge to form the long estuary of the Gironde. On the left bank of the Gironde, which at some places is almost 10 kilometers (6 miles) in width, are the vineyards of the châteaux of Médoc, from Margaux to Saint-Estèphe, producing wines with an intense yet subtle bouquet.

74 bottom For over 400 years, off the Point de Grave, opposite the mouth of the Gironde, the tall, richly decorated tower of the Cordouan lighthouse has stood in the open sea;

the building is an example of the Renaissance style on its lower floors—certainly unexpected in such a place—and of classical architecture on the upper part.

74-75 Between Bec d'Ambès and Blaye, in the middle of the estuary of the Gironde, there is a series of large islands emerging from its murky waters through which every day numerous cargo ships plough their way to the port of Bordeaux.

*76 A pleasant market town
with wide avenues and large
shady squares, standing on the
banks of the Garonne between
Bordeaux and Toulouse, Agen
is center of a prosperous
agricultural region producing
early fruit and vegetables of
all kinds—peaches, grapes and,
of course, plums, from which
the famous Agen prunes are
obtained.*

*77 The idea of building a
canal to link the Atlantic to
the Mediterranean dates from
Roman times. However, it was
not until the 17th century that,
thanks to the obstinacy of
Pierre-Paul Riquet, a Langue-
docian baron, the Canal du
Midi (seen here) was finally
constructed. It took 14 years to
build and numerous difficulties
had to be overcome between*
*Toulouse and Sète, a distance
of 240 kilometers (149 miles),
due to the very irregular
terrain: aqueducts, canal
bridges, tunnels and staircase
locks all attest to Riquet's
great ingenuity. Abandoned at
the end of the 19th century,
the Canal du Midi has enjoyed
a revival due to the popularity
of canal cruises today: the
journey lasts about a week.*

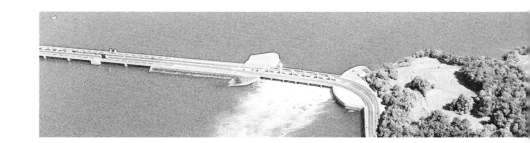

78 The great dam extending for 750 meters (2,460 feet) across the estuary of the Rance—in the magnificent setting of Dinard and Saint-Malo—supplies tidal power to a hydroelectric station generating the equivalent of the electricity consumed by a city the size of Rennes (195,000 inhabitants).

79 An excursion in a hot-air balloon over the Dôme Mountains and their magnificent landscapes. Dominating Clermont-Ferrand with its 1,465 meters (4,806 feet), the Puy de Dôme is the oldest and highest volcano of the range of puys (112 extinct volcanoes extending for 30 kilometers or 18 miles) and it was here that the scholar and scientist Blaise Pascal carried out his famous experiment to prove that air has weight.

80–81 and 82–83. Landscapes of Upper Normandy, in the Pays de Caux, by the coast. The population of this fertile region, with its vast plains where cereals are grown and cattle are reared, lives in hamlets scattered over the plateau. Here and there, in fields bordering the sea, there are remains of the concrete blockhouses built by the Germans during the Second World War as part of the famous "Atlantic Wall," which, fortunately, was less effective than foreseen. These are the colors of the Pays de Caux: the surface of the plateau is dominated by the yellow ochre of the ploughed land, the pale green of the fields of rape and beet; on the coast, as in a geological section, the high cliffs reveal the grayish white of the chalky rocks, the detritus of which continues to accumulate below, by the sea.

84–85 and 85 bottom
Vineyards and orchards
alternate for dozens of miles
in the pleasant countryside of
the Rhône valley, turning it
into a marvelous cornucopia.
Terraced, as on the west
bank between Vienne and
Tain l'Hermitage, or on both
banks, as around Orange,
the vineyards are among the
oldest in France—some were
planted by the veterans of
the Roman legions stationed
in this area. With the generic
name of Côtes-du-Rhône,
they produce strong,
generous wines such as those
of the Côte-Rotie and, above
all, Châteauneuf-du-Pape.
On the east bank, heading
southward toward Provence,
the plain between the river
and the foothills of the
mountains is covered with
orchards of peach, cherry,
pear and apricot trees. In
spring, when it becomes a
sea of pink and white
blossom, the valley resembles
a huge garden.

85 top The prosperity of the Rhône valley is not only the result of its agricultural production. The Rhône-Alpes region is one of the leading industrial areas in France: at Donzère-Mondragon, near Pierrelatte and Bollêne, where there was already a large hydroelectric power station, the nuclear establishment of Tricastin has been constructed.

86 top In the heart of the Touraine countryside, the castle of Langeais is a typical late medieval fortress: built in the fifteenth century by Louis XI, it has remained unchanged since then, in a remarkable state of preservation.

86 bottom On a fortified spur rising sheer above the Loire, the château of Saumur appears to be, curiously enough, a cross between a medieval fortress and a country house. This impression is doubtless due to the elegance of its vaulted towers and Gothic windows, the sculptures on its machicolation and, above all, the light, almost luminous color of the stone, typical of the Loire valley.

86–87 And this is
Chambord. Over and above
the magnificent architecture
of the building, the visitor
is impressed by the splendor
of the setting, superbly royal
in character: an immense
park (5,500 hectares or
13,590 acres), intended to
cater for the French kings'
passion for hunting. In order
to create lakes worthy of

this site, Francis I even
wanted to divert the Loire
(10 kilometers or 6 miles
away): since this proved to
be impossible, he decided to
alter the course of a small
river, the Cosson, turning it
into a straight canal that
was the perfect expression
of the ideal of sovereignty of
the absolute monarch.

88 bottom Amboise, on the Loire, is an epitome of Renaissance history: it calls to mind the sumptuous banquets held by Francis I, who spent his childhood here, Leonardo da Vinci, who spent his last years nearby, and the atrocities of the wars of religion. On a sunny day in summer or autumn, nothing, however, seems to disturb the soft light of this delightful spot or its peaceful fascination.

88 top Built by Louis IX (St Louis) in the thirteenth century, but associated by the Angevins with their "bon roi René," the castle of Angers dominates the Maine with its seventeen round towers and walls extending for over a kilometer. Splendid gardens have been laid out in the courtyards and in the deep moats at the foot of the towers in order to soften the austere character of the fortress with a little Angevin douceur.

88–89 Not far from Angers, the château of Serrant is a magnificent princely residence, a model of the successful combination of Renaissance and classical architecture. A legacy of the Middle Ages, the towers and moats of this country house soon lost their defensive function, serving only to enhance the view.

90 Here it was not necessary to divert a river, as at Chambord: Chenonceaux was actually built over the Cher! Constructed at the beginning of the sixteenth century, it is above all the "château des dames": Diane de Poitiers, the mistress of King Henry II, Catherine de Médicis, his wife and queen of France, and others besides have left their mark on this enchanting spot, one of the most delightful in the Loire valley.

91 The rivalry between Diane de Poitiers and Catherine de Médicis is even evident in the layout of the gardens extending along the banks of the Cher. This is Diane's garden, with the lawn divided by four paths to form the eight points of a star. On the other side of the river is Catherine's garden (partly visible in the previous photograph).

92–93 *For those arriving at Chinon from the south there is this splendid view of the ruins of the great fortress dominating the Vienne and the old town. The birthplace of Rabelais and famous for its excellent wine ("Always drink, you will never die"), Chinon had its moment of glory in the Middle Ages. It was here that in 1429 Joan of Arc came to announce to the "noble dauphin" that he was to be crowned king of France and the English would finally be driven out of his kingdom. Chinon is now a small town typifying the charm of Touraine, the real "garden of France," as Rabelais called it.*

93 top Another royal residence in the Loire valley: Blois, with its fascinating past. The château, the external walls of which have recently been restored to their original whiteness, is a masterpiece of Renaissance architecture; the great staircase with an ornamental balustrade added to the façade by Francis I is rightly famous.

93 bottom The Loire valley is rich in châteaux of all types: from the Renaissance onward, the imposing medieval fortresses were replaced by splendid country residences large and small, pleasure-houses around which there was always a park with meticulously kept parterres and flowering shrubs.

94 top The vast expanses of
Beauce with its remarkably
fertile silty soil; it is the
agricultural region par
excellence, with huge areas
devoted to the cultivation of
wheat, maize and rape.
94 bottom Around Orléans
there are still remnants of the
enormous forest in which the
kings of France used to go
hunting. The aerial view of
this farmhouse completely
isolated on its patch of
cultivated land in the middle
of the woods gives an idea of
what the patient work of
clearing undertaken over the
centuries, from the Middle Ages
onward, must have been like.

94–95 *Beauce, with its immense, practically treeless plains: as far as the eye can see stretch fields, ploughed or under crops. The houses in the village in the center of the photograph seem to be huddled together to leave as much space as possible for the cultivated land.*

96–97 *This rural landscape, very different from the previous one, is typical of those that are to be found in central and western France: plots of cultivated land divided up unevenly, clumps of trees here and there, and winding country lanes. But no one should be deceived by the modest farmhouse (lower left): in modern agriculture there is no longer room for small-scale farming.*

98 top With a backdrop of sun-drenched hills, located amid olives and palms, Cagnes-sur-Mer on the Côte d'Azur has a very special light year-round that has long made it popular with painters: Renoir spent his last years here and there is a museum devoted to his work. This is a view of the upper town, with its picturesque streets and flights of steps; it is reached by the Montée de la Bourgade, clearly visible in the center of the photograph.

98 bottom In the 1920s numerous artists came to spend long periods in Saint-Paul-de-Vence or settle there for good, and from then on it became one of the Meccas of the art world on the Côte d'Azur. The splendid museum of the Fondation Maeght, on the Des Gardettes hill just outside the village, is evidence of this.

98–99 In Saint-Paul-de-Vence, the ramparts built by Francis I in the sixteenth century are practically intact: they are clearly visible in the lower part of the photograph. In the center is the square tower of the old keep facing the tower of the Gothic church. Rue Grande, which crosses the whole village, is lined with numerous artist's studios and shops selling antiques and handicrafts of all kinds.

100 In the Pays Albigeois, the village of Cordes is perched on top of a hill (known locally as a peuch) from which its picturesque full name of Cordes-sur-ciel derives. Originally a medieval fortress, the village was surrounded in the thirteenth century by two fortified walls, numerous remains of which are visible here: ramparts, towers and gateways.

101 It is only relatively recently that Cordes has recovered some of its former prosperity thanks to the setting up, after the Second World War, of numerous handicrafts workshops, bringing life back to the steep winding streets of the old village and the splendid Gothic buildings that are the main attraction of Rue Droite.

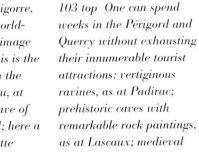

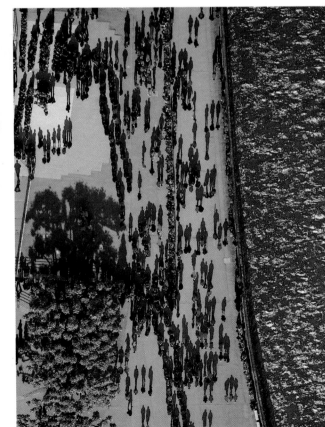

103 center In the Auvergne region, south of Clermont-Ferrand, the magnificent panorama of the extinct volcanoes known as the puys. There's nothing better than a hot-air balloon for observing them from above in all their wild beauty.

103 bottom right Every year, hoping for a miraculous cure, millions of pilgrims accompany the sick who come to Lourdes to bathe in the waters of the spring that St Bernadette caused to gush forth with her hands.

104–105 Between Avignon and Arles, the impressive ruins of the fortress of Baux-de-Provence seem to be suspended on their rocky spur, surrounded by nothing but sheer precipices. This village, the lords of which claimed to be descendants of one of the three Magi and which once had as many as four thousand inhabitants, has a turbulent past. It still lives thanks to the craftspeople who have opened their workshops here and the splendid vineyards in the surrounding countryside.

102 In the heart of Bigorre, Lourdes has been a world-famous center of pilgrimage for over a century. This is the upper church, built on the banks of the River Pau, at the point where the cave of Massabielle is located; here a peasant girl, Bernadette Soubirous, had visions of the Virgin Mary in 1858.

103 top One can spend weeks in the Périgord and Quercy without exhausting their innumerable tourist attractions: vertiginous ravines, as at Padirac; prehistoric caves with remarkable rock paintings, as at Lascaux; medieval fortresses located in spectacular surroundings, such as the castle of Beynac, seen here, overlooking the valley of the Dordogne. Not to mention the local cuisine with its superb flavors: truffles, foie gras and comfits....

106 The colors of the Midi, here close to Carcassonne in the southwest: ochre and green predominate in a sun-drenched land where the summers are always hot and dry.

107 Viticulture is one of the main resources of the Mediterranean regions of the south of France, from the plains of the Bas-Languedoc, seen here, to the valleys of the Corbières, between Narbonne and Perpignan. As regards the wine that is produced, until recently it was quantity that counted: but in the last few years an enormous effort has been made to improve the quality and so far the results have been very promising.

108–109 The marvelous patchwork of the Provençal countryside with its extremely diversified crops; the whimsical boundaries of the irregular mosaic of fields are a reminder that small-scale farming was long the rule in France.

THE CITIES WITH THE COLORS OF TIME

110 In the square in front of Notre Dame in Paris, on the Île de la Cité, visitors never tire of admiring the magnificent façade of the cathedral with its immense rose window, the gallery of kings and the three portals adorned with large numbers of statues. The whole intellectual universe of the Middle Ages—both religious and political—is represented here as in a "Bible of stone" that everyone may read, as Victor Hugo put it so eloquently in his famous novel, Notre-Dame de Paris.

111 Seen from above, the Latin-cross plan of Notre Dame is very clearly visible: over the crossing soars the richly ornamented flèche (slender spire), and it is possible to admire the extraordinary delicacy of the flying buttresses supporting the building's vault.

112 top Burnt down at the time of the Paris Commune, in 1871, the Hôtel de Ville (town hall) was immediately rebuilt on the same site; the central part of the present façade, overlooking the old Place de Grève, is a faithful copy of the original one dating from the Renaissance.

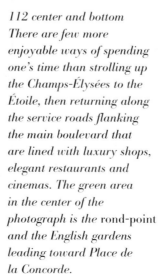

112 center and bottom There are few more enjoyable ways of spending one's time than strolling up the Champs-Élysées to the Étoile, then returning along the service roads flanking the main boulevard that are lined with luxury shops, elegant restaurants and cinemas. The green area in the center of the photograph is the rond-point and the English gardens leading toward Place de la Concorde.

113 The huge glass pyramid, designed by I.M. Pei, in the large courtyard of the Louvre, is already ten years old. As happened with the Eiffel Tower, the insertion of a work of these dimensions in a monumental context with a style that is evidently very different did not fail to arouse controversy. However, the photograph opposite is an excellent illustration of way the pyramid fits in perfectly with the geometrical forms of the Louvre courtyard.

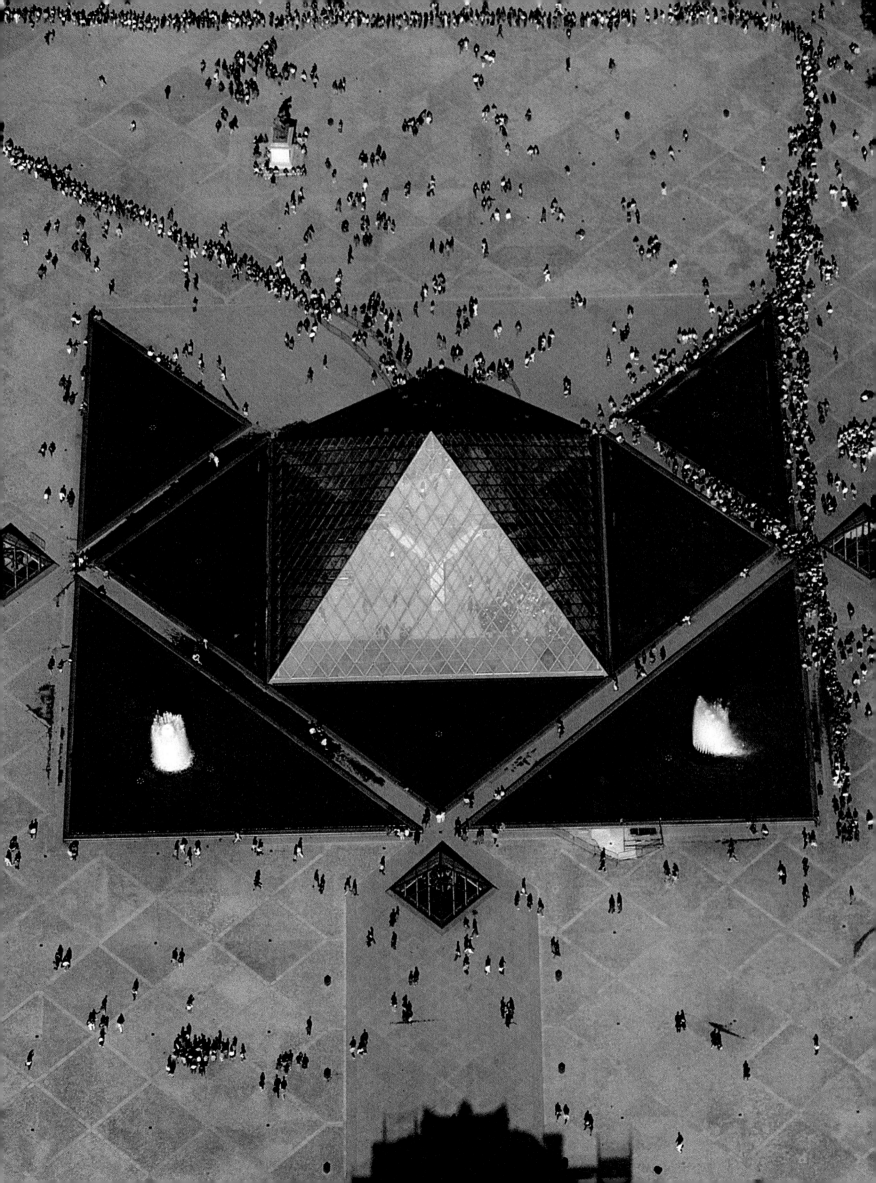

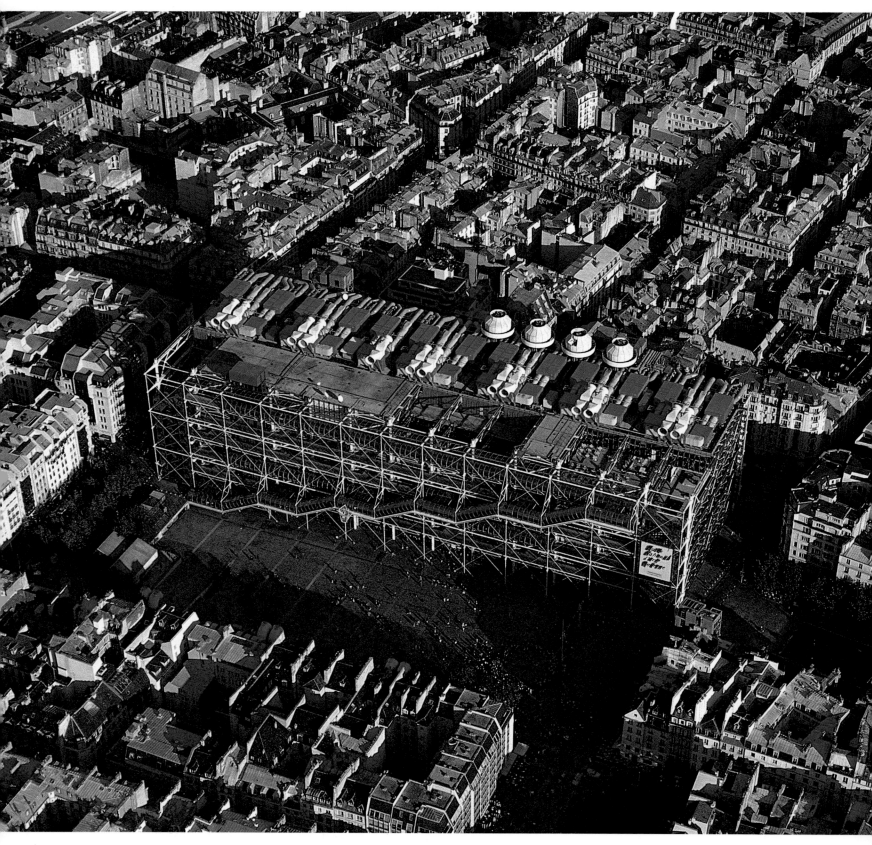

114–115 The construction of the Centre Georges Pompidou, with its avant-garde architecture, in the middle of one of the oldest quarters of Paris, seemed to be a wild gamble. But it paid off: it has drawn the crowds beyond all expectations; every year millions of visitors flock to see the exhibitions of the Musée Nationale d'Art Moderne and to participate in the numerous cultural activities at the Center, including films, lectures and concerts of contemporary music.

115 top Another recent town planning scheme: the new Opéra built along the edge of the Place de la Bastille, the very name of which is sufficient to evoke the most famous episode of the French Revolution.

115 bottom On the western side of Paris, the Défense is a striking example of modern town planning: both a residential quarter and business center where the leading multinational companies have opened their offices, the complex is built around an immense pedestrian area under which are located car parks, service roads and railway stations. In particular, the futuristic character of this project is represented by the arch, an enormous cubic structure (it could contain the cathedral of Notre Dame!) faced with glass and white Carrara marble—like the CNIT (Centre National des Industries et des Techniques) building, the triangular vault of which is visible here—of an incredible lightness.

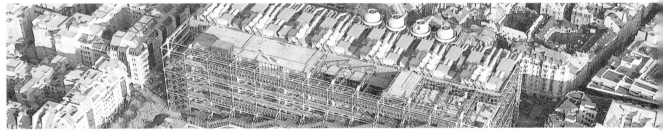

116 *Ports on the French coasts, seaside towns, pirates' hideouts: Saint-Malo is the quintessence of all this, with its ramparts, bastions and redoubts that made the peninsula where the old town is located virtually inapproachable.*

This is the birthplace of such historic figures as Jacques Cartier, the explorer of Canada, and Chateaubriand, the great romantic writer buried on the islet of Grand Bé, clearly visible here (the first off the coast).

117 *The violent fighting during the Liberation, in August 1944, almost completely destroyed Saint-Malo, except for the bastions: the center of the old town was rebuilt as it was before* *the war and the excellent results can be seen here. In the center of the photograph is the cathedral of Saint-Vincent, the Grand-Rue and the Grande Porte (city gate) flanked by two towers.*

118 top The development of Le Touquet and its huge beach (between Boulogne-sur-Mer and the Bay of Somme) as a tourist resort began in the nineteenth century. The "Enduro des sables," a famous motorcycle race designed to test endurance on the sand, takes place here every year in mid-February.

118–119 Calais is certainly better known as a port than for the attractions of its beach. Nonetheless, there is a large beach with every amenity to the west of the port entrance; behind it the sea wall serves as a pleasant promenade.

119 top Situated at about forty kilometers (25 miles) from the English coast, Calais has always been the main port for trade with Britain. At present it is the leading port in France for passenger traffic—the ferries linking Calais and Dover carry millions of people very year—and the commercial port is also very busy.

119 bottom The other large port in northern France is Dunkirk. This is the Hôtel de Ville (town hall), with its central tower, facing the Bassin de Commerce where pleasure boats are moored. In 1940 the huge sand-dunes extending north of the town were the scene of one the most dramatic episodes of the Second World War—the evacuation of the British troops from France under constant attack from German planes.

120–121 In the futuristic profusion of motorway interchanges and slip-roads, heavy lorries arriving from all over Europe head toward the Channel Tunnel terminal, south of Calais.

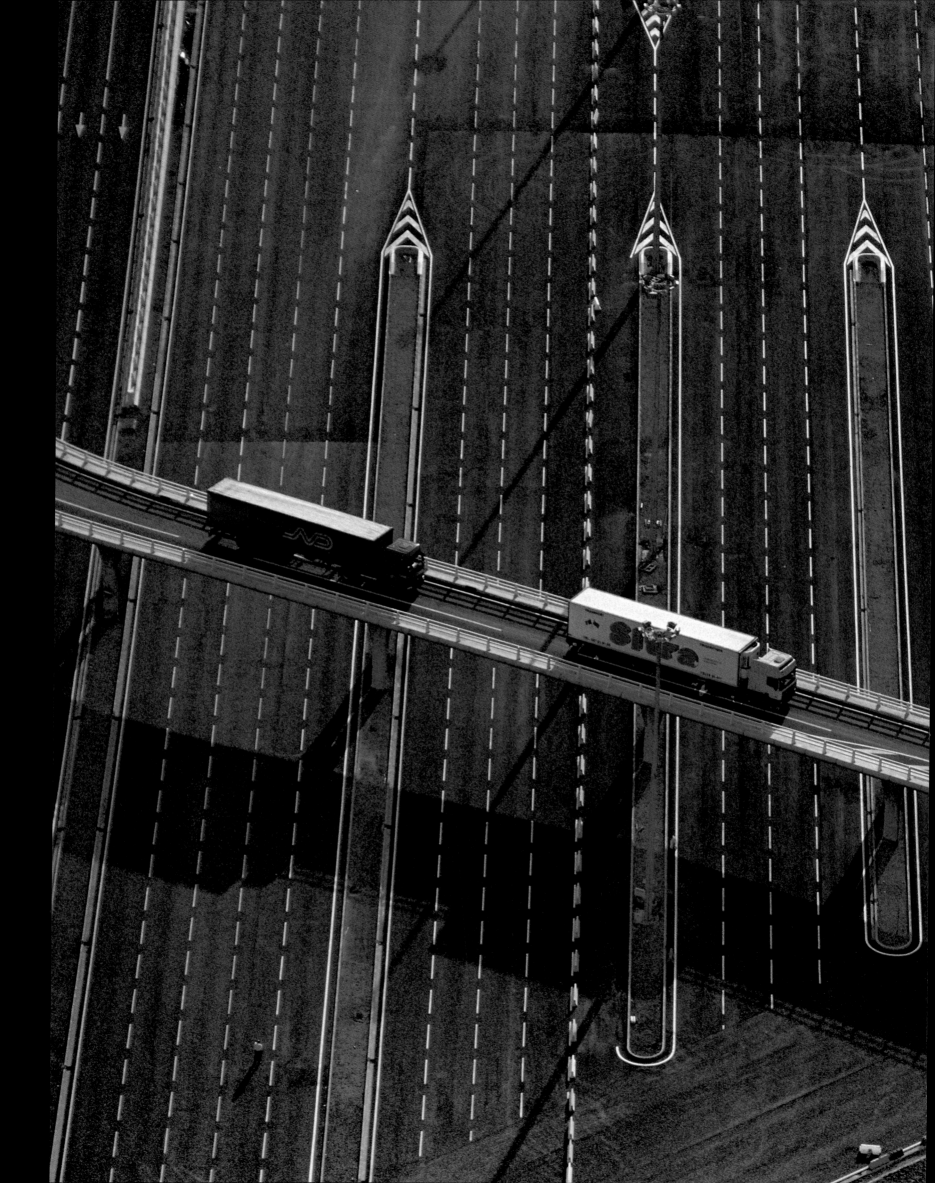

122 top At about a hundred kilometers (62 miles) from the estuary of the Seine, Rouen is a large port, for both sea and river traffic, an important industrial city and capital of Haute-Normandie.

The old town, on the north bank of the river, has been splendidly restored and the cathedral is rightly considered to be one the most outstanding examples of French Gothic architecture.

122–123 A close-up of the docks at Calais. The leading port in France for passenger traffic, Calais also handles large quantities of goods: here, on the left, is the dock able to contain huge ships carrying all types of cargo.

123 top and bottom The magnificent arcaded façades of the houses in the Grand Place in Arras are typical examples of seventeenth- and eighteenth-century Flemish architecture, as are the Hôtel de Ville and its imposing tower 75 meters (246 feet) in height bottom. This town, which was very prosperous in the Middle Ages and was seriously damaged in the First World War, is also associated with Robespierre, one of the leading figures of the French Revolution, who was born here in 1758.

124 top Situated on the River Meurthe, near Nancy, Saint-Nicolas-du-Port, now merely a small industrial town, boasts this magnificent basilica in Flamboyant style, a major center of pilgrimage in the Middle Ages.

124 center Former the capital of the duchy of Brittany, Nantes is a large port located at the head of the long estuary of the Loire leading to the Atlantic. It is a city that has a charm all its own that was particularly appreciated by surrealist poet André Breton and film director Jacques Demy.

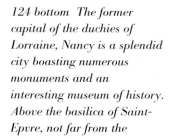

124 bottom The former capital of the duchies of Lorraine, Nancy is a splendid city boasting numerous monuments and an interesting museum of history. Above the basilica of Saint-Epvre, not far from the

famous Place Stanislas, with its gilded wrought iron railings, the Place de la Carrière is visible; with its classical proportions, it was formerly used as a drill ground and for equestrian parades.

125 A masterpiece of Gothic architecture, Chartres is perhaps the most impressive cathedral of them all: when entering the building, the visitor feels— also in a physical sense—the

majesty of the monumental space populated by the thousands of figures represented here, including five thousand on the stained-glass windows alone.

126 top The façade of Reims Cathedral is one of the most beautiful in France, especially for the astonishing richness of its sculptures. Besides the gallery of kings, above the rose window, the three portals, giving access to the nave and the aisles flanking it, are adorned with innumerable statues portraying the main figures of the Old and New Testaments. On the south portal is the famous Smiling Angel, *the grace of which never ceases to astound visitors.*

126 bottom and 126–127. Noted above all for its superb monuments, Reims is also a large modern city that, together with Épernay, is the capital of champagne: Pommery, Taittinger, Veuve Cliquot-Ponsardin, Piper-Heidsieck, Mümm, Ruinart, Moët et Chandon—these are names known all over the world. Naturally, one can tour the vast vineyards extending over the surrounding countryside, but in Reims it is also possible to visit the immense cellars in the Champ de Mars district and on the slopes of the Saint-Nicolas hill: the majority of the leading brands of champagne have had their premises here since the end of the eighteenth century.

128–129. The Île d'Oléron is the largest island off the Atlantic coast of France. The ideal place for family holidays, it offers plentiful sunshine, iodine-rich ocean air, the splendid sandy beaches of Saint-Trojan and forests of maritime pines. This is the Château-d'Oléron, the old fortress that during Louis XIV's reign was intended to protect the mouth of the Charente.

130–131 As this splendid view of the old port demonstrates, La Rochelle is undoubtedly the most picturesque city of the Atlantic coast between Nantes and Bordeaux. In the summer it is very pleasant to stroll along its quays dominated by the towers guarding the entrance to the port and, in the city center, in the streets flanked by arcades. The siege of La Rochelle, a city with a strong Protestant tradition, in 1627–28, was one of the most dramatic episodes in the French civil wars.

132 top Off the coast near La Rochelle and recently linked to the mainland by a long bridge, the Île de Ré is a popular holiday island. In effect, the "île blanche," as it has been called because of its low, brilliantly white houses, offers everything one could wish for: sunbathing on wide sandy beaches, walks to the old salterns or in the pinewoods, or else to the old fortress of Saint-Martin, designed by Vauban, which is seen here and is now a delightful holiday village.

132 bottom The village of Ars-en-Ré with, in the center of the photograph, the slender steeple of the church of Saint-Étienne; this is painted black and white to serve as a landmark for ships sailing off the coast.

133 The port of Saint-Martin-de Ré. The sailing ships that used to come here to load the salt and wine produced on the island have been replaced by pleasure craft and the occasional fishing boat.

134–135. At the foot of the last offshoots of the Pyrenees, near the Spanish border, Collioure is undoubtedly the most picturesque of the Catalan ports of the Côte Vermeille: the contrast and vividness of the colors—the red of the tiles, the blue of the sky and sea, the green of the foliage—are very different here from those of the Côte d'Azur.

136-137 Situated in a region of the south of France that has little in common with the areas bordering the Mediterranean, Bordeaux is very different from the other major cities in the country. It is characterized by ironical distrust with regard to the central government and its authoritarianism, a long-standing tradition of international trade, especially with Britain and the Americas, and a taste for the good things in life that is perfectly expressed by the excellent quality of the wines produced in the area. Stendhal affirmed that Bordeaux was "unquestionably the most beautiful city in France," and with good reason.

*137 top and bottom
Situated on a loop in the
Doubs, dominated by an
enormous rocky spur,
Besançon was for a long
time a city of great strategic
importance, as the huge
citadel built in the
seventeenth century
demonstrates so
spectacularly. The town
gradually developed on both
banks of the river: fairly
recently, the watch industry
made a major contribution to
its prosperity, as did artificial
silk—rayon—which was
invented here at the end of
the nineteenth century.*

138 top The three Ponts Couverts (covered bridges) over the River Ill in Strasbourg, the towers of which formed part of the medieval walls, mark the limits of the Petite France quarter, one of the most picturesque and best preserved districts of the old town.

138–139 A panoramic view of the old center of Strasbourg, built on an island located between two branches of the River Ill (on the left and right of the photograph). In the foreground are the three Ponts Couverts (once they really were covered) and the Petite France quarter.

138 bottom Built of the red stone of the Vosges, the cathedral of Notre Dame in Strasbourg, with its single steeple in an unusual style. On the façade, now splendidly restored, there is a great variety of sculptures, both statues and bas-reliefs.

139 top Together with Brussels and Luxembourg, Strasbourg is one of the capitals of modern Europe: it is, in fact, the seat of the European Parliament (seen in the photograph), as well as of numerous other institutions, such as the European Human Rights Court.

140–141 Chalon-sur-Saône
is a river port excellently
sited at the confluence
between the Saône and the
Canal du Centre and at the
point where various trade
routes intersect. Together
with old houses clustered
round the cathedral of
Saint-Vincent (upper left in
the photograph), the island
in the foreground is one of
the most picturesque areas
of the city.

141 top In the summer, as they head southward along the Autoroute du Soleil in the direction of Provence and the Côte d'Azur, it is only after passing Valence—the center of which may be seen in the photograph—that impatient holiday-makers feel they have finally crossed the threshold of what is known as the Midi.

141 center Situated in the Marne valley, Château-Thierry is the birthplace of the poet Jean de la Fontaine, noted for his Fables; a museum is devoted to him in the mansion where he was born in 1621, not far from the Grande Rue, which forms a curve in the photograph, skirting the hill surmounted by a castle.

142–143 The splendid position of Cahors: the city is located in a loop of the Lot, which for a long time made it practically inexpugnable. On the left is the famous Valentré bridge, with its three tall machicolated towers that controlled the river crossing.

144-145 Vienne, on the banks of the Rhône, with its splendid light and fascinating history. This old Gallo-Roman city has numerous ancient monuments: the Roman theatre, now completely excavated, could hold about 14,000 people;

every summer an important Jazz Festival takes place here. It is also an old Christian city: here, near the suspension bridge, is the cathedral of Saint-Maurice in which Romanesque and Gothic elements are blended in perfect harmony.

145 top On the vast reservoirs serving the Canal du Centre and lakes to the south and east of the town, Le Creusot was, for a long time, one of the jewels of the French metallurgical industry, symbolized by the enormous drop hammer now displayed at a crossroads. For over a century and a half the whole region was under the sway of the Schneider family, an ancestor of which, Eugène, a master blacksmith, settled in Le Creusot in 1836. The blast furnaces have now been shut down, but the town is still an important industrial center.

144 bottom and 145 bottom From two different viewpoints, the tip of the island of Chalon-sur-Rhône, with the Tour du Doyenné and large hospital, most of which was built in the seventeenth century.

146–147 The least that one can say is that citadel of Carcassonne, as well as being the largest in Europe, is very impressive: it is as if one had suddenly been whisked back to the Middle Ages, to the Age of Chivalry. This impression is due above all to the remarkable restoration of the whole town carried out by the architect Eugène Emmanuel Viollet-le-Duc in the nineteenth century, with exemplary care being taken over the historical details.

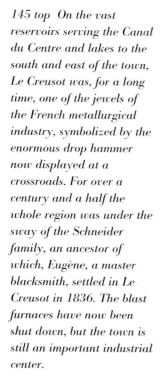

145

*148 top The magnificent
roofs of glazed multicolored
tiles are a special feature of
Dijon and the surrounding
area: a splendid example is
visible here, near the
cathedral of Saint-Bénigne,
an ancient abbey church in
the typical Gothic style of
Burgundy.*

*148 center Not far from the
Palace of the Dukes and
States of Burgundy, the
church of Saint-Michel is
built in a mixture of styles:
started at the end of the
fifteenth century, it was only
completed a century and a
half later. The Flamboyant
style of the first stage of its
construction is also found in
the interior of the church
and is particularly evident
in the remarkable height of
the choir.*

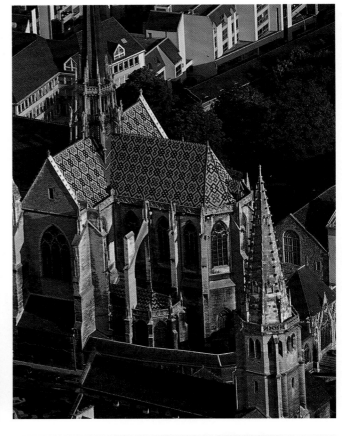

*148 bottom left The
splendid façade of the
twelfth-century church of
Saint-Philibert, near the
cathedral of Saint-Bénigne.*

*149 In the center of the
photograph, opposite the
semicircular square designed
by Jules Hardouin-Mansart—
the architect in charge of
building at Versailles from
1678 onward—stands the
Palace of the Dukes and
States of Burgundy, which*
*now houses the excellent art
gallery. The capital of a
thriving region, above all due
to the splendid vineyards
that are cultivated to the
south of the city, Dijon is a
prosperous city where it is
well worth stopping off for
lunch or dinner!*

151 Évian-les-Bains is the other important resort and spa town on the French side of Lake Geneva. Not only is it more famous and fashionable than Thonon but its waters are universally known for their dietetic and therapeutic qualities: they may be drunk, or visitors can even bathe in them; practically tasteless, they are very good for one's health.

151 center In the center of the photograph is the church of Saint Hippolyte in Thonon, where St Francis of Sales came to preach at the end of the sixteenth century in order to restore Catholicism to a province where Protestantism was rife.

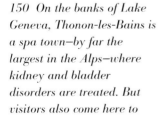

151 bottom The harbor of Lorient, in the south of Brittany, has long contained an important submarine base. Totally destroyed in the Second World War, the town was reconstructed with interesting modern buildings, such as the church of Saint-Louis and the Maison de la Mer.

152–153 By the time the Rhône reaches Avignon, the valley is adorned with all the colors of Provence. The famous bridge is clearly visible here, as is the papal palace, which provides a splendid setting for the most important events of the theatre festival that draws huge crowds every summer.

150 On the banks of Lake Geneva, Thonon-les-Bains is a spa town—by far the largest in the Alps—where kidney and bladder disorders are treated. But visitors also come here to enjoy the attractions—in particular, the delightful gardens—of a small lakeside resort set in splendid scenery. Opposite, on the other side of the lake, is Switzerland.

154–155 Every year, in the heart of the Camargue, between the étangs de Launes and de l'Impérial, during the fête of Saintes-Maries-de-la-Mer, in May, gypsies make the pilgrimage to pay homage to their patron saint, Sara, the black servant of the two Maries—Mary, sister of the Virgin and wife of Cleopas, and Mary Salome, mother of the apostles James the Greater and John the Evangelist—who it is said came to seek refuge here in the Camargue after the death of Christ.

155 top It is the fortified church, in the center of the photograph, that the relics of the three saints are jealously guarded, as is the little blue boat that the pilgrims carry in procession to the sea.

155 bottom The fêtes of horses and bulls are part of the traditions of the Camargue: the Saintes-Maries also have their bullrings, such as Arles and Nîmes.

156–157 *It was here that, on two occasions (1248 and 1270), St Louis (Louis IX) embarked for the Crusades: at the time Aigues-Mortes was linked directly to the sea by a canal, the Grau Louis. But the relentless silting up of the channels leading to deep water caused the decline of town, which in its heyday had as many as 15,000 inhabitants. With its fortified walls that have survived intact, Aigues-Mortes is still a superb reminder of those distant times.*

157 bottom The Tour de Constance is an imposing circular keep dating from the period of St Louis that guarded the entrance to the port. Subsequently it was used for the detention of political prisoners of all sorts. Reaching a height of forty meters, its turret commands a magnificent view of the surrounding area.

158 top On the Gulf of Lions, between the immense Étang de Thau and the Mediterranean, the harbor at Sète is certainly one the most picturesque that one could imagine. Such contrasting figures as Paul Valéry and Georges Bresson have sung the praises of this sun-drenched town where

they were born. But it is their neighbor from Narbonne, Charles Trenet, who is the author of one of the finest songs ever written about the sea: "La mer qu'on voit danser / Le long des golfs clairs..." (The sea dancing before one's eyes / In the bright bays...).

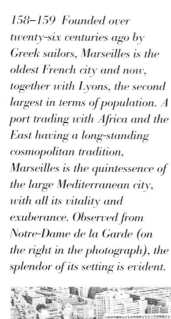

158–159 Founded over twenty-six centuries ago by Greek sailors, Marseilles is the oldest French city and now, together with Lyons, the second largest in terms of population. A port trading with Africa and the East having a long-standing cosmopolitan tradition, Marseilles is the quintessence of the large Mediterranean city, with all its vitality and exuberance. Observed from Notre-Dame de la Garde (on the right in the photograph), the splendor of its setting is evident.

159 top Outside Marseilles harbor, just a quarter of an hour away by boat, stands the castle of If, made famous by Alexandre Dumas' novel, The Count of Monte Cristo, from which the hero, Edmont Dantès, unjustly imprisoned for years in the appalling dungeons of the castle, manages to escape: naturally, after he has had so long to ponder over it, his revenge will be terrible....

159 bottom This is the fortified entrance to the old port of Marseilles, now reserved for pleasure boats. The docks of the modern port are sited further west.

160 top Although it is not far from the port and its congestion, the small cove of La Glaye, between the Tour du Portalet and the Tour Vieille, has preserved all the charm of Saint-Tropez as it was before the tourist invasion.

160 bottom South of Saint-Tropez, the large beaches of Pampelonne and Tahiti are close to Ramatuelle, a delightful Provençal village perched on a hill amid vineyards.

*160–161 The port of
Saint-Tropez, with yachts
of all nationalities: those
wishing to enjoy the
peaceful atmosphere
conveyed by the
photograph should go there
early in the morning! In the
summer, the hustle and
bustle of this place
resembles that of a funfair.*

*161 bottom The view over
the Bay of Saint-Tropez
and beyond to the Maures
and the Estérel from the top
of the keep of the citadel, to
the east of the town, is worth
the journey: it is sufficient
to make visitors forget the
traffic jams and crowds that
they have had to put up
with in order to get there.*

162–163 Do the inhabitants of Menton really know the meaning of the word "winter"? Probably not. Orange and lemon trees and tropical flowers grow year round and the Promenade du Soleil, skirting the beach and the old town to the Quai Napoléon (seen here in the foreground), lives up to its name in all seasons.

*163 top With its
pinewoods, cypresses
and mimosa shrubs, Cap
Martin (west of Menton)
is a delightful spot.*

*163 bottom Along the path
following the whole of the
west side of the promontory
of Cap Martin there are
superb views of Monaco,*
*the headland of Cap
Ferrat and Roquebrune,
an old village perched
on the hillside overlooking
the bay.*

164 top Between Cap Ferrat and Cap de Nice, the harbor of Villefranche-sur-Mer, with its deep waters, is one of the most beautiful places on the Riviera, with the corniche roads built into the mountainside on three levels hundreds of feet above the sea between Nice and Menton. At Villefranche, the chapel of Saint-Pierre, decorated by Jean Cocteau in the fifties, is also worth a visit.

164 center Cap Ferrat is a wonderful place indeed: houses and villas amid the pines, parks and gardens, it's all so delightful, in summer and winter alike. It is possible to explore it on the path hugging the rocky coast of the promontory for about ten kilometers (6 miles).

164 bottom Antibes: this was the Greek city of Antipolis which was founded in the 4th c. BC. Antipolis means "the city in front," in this case in front of Nice which was the other city in the Bay of Angels. In spite of everything, the large modern triangular buildings are integrated into the landscape. Preferable, however, is Grimaldi Castle in the old city which houses a

museum dedicated to Picasso and other collections of contemporary art.

165 The old town of Menton, with the splendid Baroque church of Saint-Michel, the colors of which, yellow and pale green, recall those of the cathedral of Saint-Réparate in the center of Nice and nearby Italy.

166–167 The rocky headland of Monaco and the Oceanographic Museum built on the cliffs towering above the sea. Beyond the harbor, the modern buildings of Monte Carlo seem to be launching an attack on the surrounding hills.

168 top Dominated by a hill on top of which there was formerly a fortress, the port of Nice is mainly used by the ferry service to Corsica, but cruise ships also stop here: the fifth largest city in France, Nice is in great demand as a port of call.

168–169 Every year, in May, Cannes is synonymous with the International film Festival, with its Croisette promenade between the beach and the luxury hotels. But it also has a harbor with busy quays and, above, the old town on the slopes of Mont Chavalier—the "Suquet" as it is known in Cannes.

169 top This panoramic view of Cannes highlights the importance of the harbor, where fishing boats mingle with yachts, some of them very luxurious indeed. In the last hundred years, in fact, the town has become one of the most fashionable resorts in Europe, visited by royalty, aristocracy and millionaires of all nationalities.

169 bottom Facing the Baie des Anges, along the Promenade des Anglais, the name of which reveals the popularity of the Côte d'Azur with the British aristocracy in the nineteenth century, luxury establishments alternate with sumptuous hotels, such as the ones seen here, the Negresco Hotel and the old Ruhl casino.

170 top The citadel built when the Genoese controlled the harbor of Saint-Florent, in the large bay overlooked by the west side of Cap Corse. Nearby, between Saint-Florent and Calvi, there is a series of deserted beaches and coves on the rocky coast washed by a clear blue sea, while the interior is dominated by towering crags (maquis of Nebbio and Agriates)—in short, Corsica is truly the "Île de Beauté."

170 center and bottom Situated in a delightful small bay on the west coats, Calvi is the Corsican town closest to Nice and the Côte d'Azur. Every year in June a very special jazz festival takes place here: about two hundred musicians perform for a week, not just in organized concerts, but at all times of day and night, in cafés, restaurants and on the beach. Nobody is paid: all they receive is free accommodation, and they just play for the fun of it. The late lamented pianist Michel Petrucciani was a regular visitor to the Calvi festival.

171 The high town of Calvi, with its walls reinforced by bastions and the palace of the Genoese governors, dating from the fifteenth century. It is also possible to visit the remains of a house where Christopher Columbus is said to have been born: at the time Calvi was under Genoese rule, so why not?

172 top Between the quarters of Terra Vecchia and Terra Nova lies the old port of Bastia—Bastia the proud, the reserved, the discreet: proud of its past and its charms, perhaps more secret than elsewhere. It's pleasant to sit under the palms of an evening in Place Saint-Nicolas, seen in the upper part of the photograph.

173 top left Here at Bastia, on the heights of Terra Nova, is the cathedral of Sainte-Marie, inside which there are splendid Baroque decorations.

173 top right The rugged mountain landscapes of the interior of Corsica hold a very special fascination for the visitor. This is Corte, the cultural capital of the island and its citadel with eight bastions perched on the edge of sheer precipices towering over the Tavignano valley.

172 bottom and 172–173 On the west coast of Corsica, Ajaccio extends along a huge bay where there are magnificent views. Not only is it the birthplace of Napoleon but also that of Tino Rossi, who became famous in the 1930s in a very different field: the serenade and operetta. Ajaccio is now the capital of the region of Corsica.

LA MER QU'ON VOIT DANSER

(the dancing sea)

174 Opened in 1995, the Ponte de Normandie is the third of the great bridges (the other two are those of Tancarville and Brotonne) linking the opposite banks of the lower Seine. A masterpiece of modern technology, this cable-stayed bridge, over two kilometers (1 miles) in length, also has aesthetic appeal, as this superb aerial photograph shows.

175 In the extreme north of Normandy, on the border with Picardy, the high cliffs of Le Tréport overlook a long shingle beach. Located at the mouth of a small river, the Bresle, the quays of the fishing port come alive in the summer.

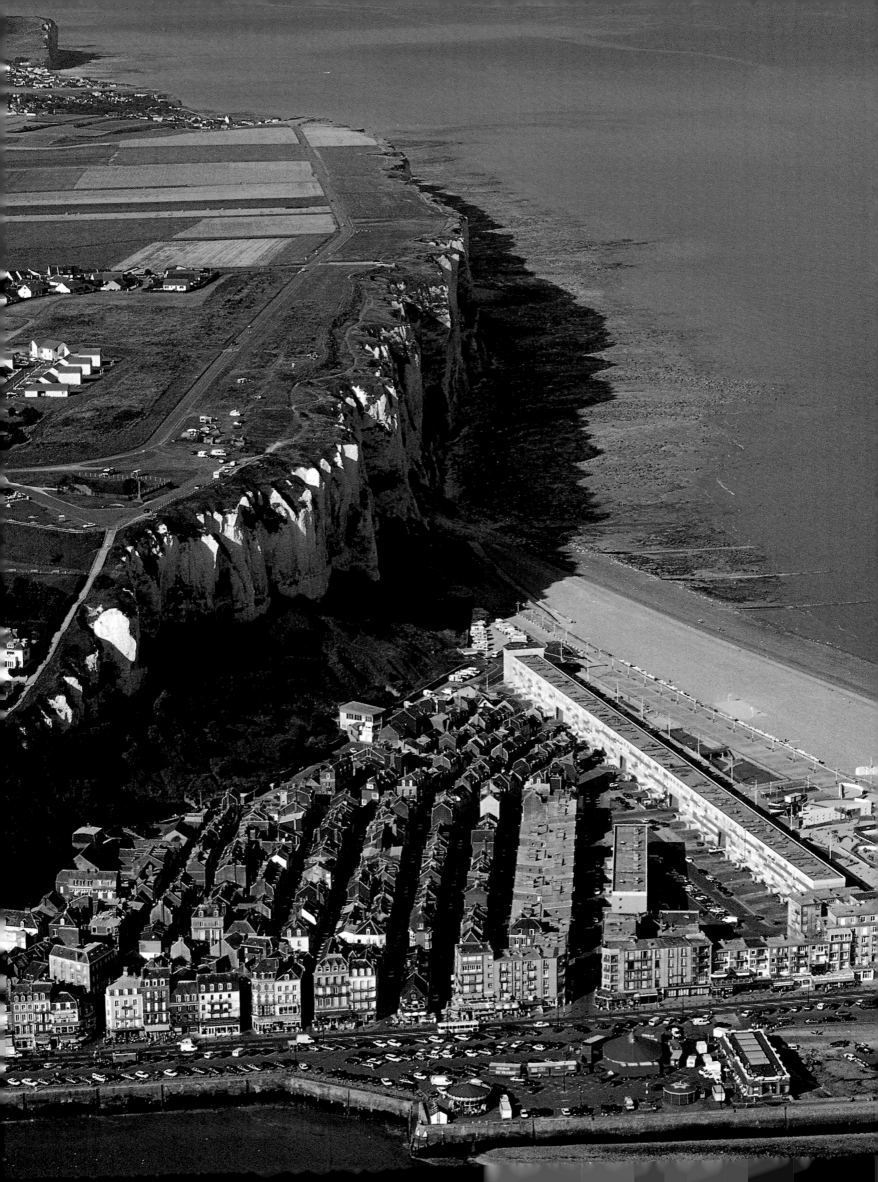

176 top A typical view of the Pays de Caux, with lush meadows going right up to the sea, with waves breaking against the cliffs about 70 meters (230 feet) below. However used you are to it, this landscape always creates a strange impression, all the more so because of the wind, which blows here in sharp gusts.

176 bottom The Côte d'Albâtre, the high chalk cliffs of which form the spectacular seaward limit of the Pays de Caux, is also characterized by steep-sided valleys where small fishing ports or seaside resorts are situated: a typical example is Étretat, seen in the center of the photograph in the hollow between the Falaise d'Amont and the Falaise d'Aval.

176-177 *Étretat and the Falaise d'Aval. In the foreground is the elegant arch of the Porte d'Aval and the Aiguille (70 meters or 230 feet in height); in the right background is the larger arch of Manneporte. The sea and wind have sculpted these fantastic forms that have always fascinated painters and writers, in particular Maupassant, who spent his childhood at Étretat.*

178–179 *The column in the center of the photograph commemorates the first flight across the English Channel made by Louis Blériot in 1909.*

180-181 The magnificent landscape of the Bay of Somme where there are vast expanses of sand with delicate colors and rivulets of water left behind by the sea at low tide. Here, in the northern part of the bay, is Le Crotoy, with its small port specializing in coastal fishing (the principal catches include prawns and herrings). The pleasure craft seen here are a reminder that Le Crotoy is also a delightful seaside resort particularly suitable for family holidays.

180 bottom left A little further north of Boulogne, the immense sandy and shingly beach of Wimereux heralds the high dunes bordering the coastal road leading toward Cap Gris-Nez.

180 bottom right Situated on the south side of the Bay of Somme, opposite Le Crotoy, Saint-Valery is another picturesque fishing port. But the whole bay is of great interest: its progressive silting up has made it a nature reserve particularly rich in fish and migratory birds (over 300 species of the latter have been counted). Hunting is a traditional sport here, although, for ecological reasons, this poses many problems today.

181 top right The port of Dieppe, on the coast of Upper Normandy, has long benefited from the fact that it is the closest to Paris, and it is still very important today. This is a view of the recently completed marina.

181 bottom Between Cap Gris-Nez and Wimereux, the old naval port of Ambleteuse was protected by a fort built by Vauban. Now families come here to spend the day on its beach backed by sand-dunes.

182–183 and 184–185 Outside the Bay of Mont-Saint-Michel, off the peninsula of Cotentin, near Granville, lies the archipelago of the Chausey Islands, a multitude of small islands (about fifty), most of which are minute. According to legend they are the remains of an ancient forest that was swallowed up by the sea a long time ago. The largest island, known as the Grande Île, is the only inhabited one (just over a hundred people stay there in the summer) and can be partially visited, while the rest of the archipelago is private. In the Middle Ages there were quarries on the islands from which the granite used to build Mont-Saint-Michel was extracted. As may be seen in these splendid photographs, the area is particularly fascinating for the wild beauty of its most isolated points, only accessible to small boats. At low tide huge stretches of sand are exposed: but visitors must take care not to be caught unawares when the tide comes in again!

186–187 The oyster-beds of Marennes form an enormous labyrinth that extends for miles along both sides of the mouth of the Seudre. Green oysters, the speciality of Marennes, with their particularly delicate flavor, are cultivated here; their color may be seen in the aerial views on these pages.

188–189 The western tip of the Île de Ré, facing the open sea. In the center of the photograph is the lighthouse of the Baleines and, on the left, the large bay of the same name bordered by sand-dunes where whales used to beach. In the upper part of the photograph are the bluish pans of the old salterns, now a nature reserve.

190 top, 190 bottom and
192–193 The salterns of the
Île d'Oléron, on the east
coast, have been converted
into oyster-farms, which,
together with fishing, are one
of the island's main
resources.

190–191 Like the Île de Ré,
the Île d'Oléron is very low-
lying. The Pointe de
Chassiron, the lighthouse of
which is visible on the right
of the photograph, is
something of an exception

because it is bordered by low
cliffs. On the west side of the
island the Côte Sauvage is
exposed to the full force of
the Atlantic waves, which
break violently on the beach
as soon as the wind gets up.

194–195 South-west of Bordeaux, on the edge of the forest of the Landes, the Bassin d'Arcachon is an immense bay 250 square kilometers (97 square miles) in area. The bed of this is exposed at low tide, forming enormous sandbanks between which the water continues to flow.

196 In the center Bassin d'Arcachon, the Île aux Oiseaux is one of the few islands in the bay to emerge from the water even at high tide. It is still possible to see two fishermen's houses built on piles (these are known as tchanquées, because in Guascon tchanque means stilt). Here, amidst the modern pleasure craft, there is a pinasse, the boat traditionally used by the oyster-farmers in the bay.

197 top left Arachon is the main seaside resort in the bay and the center of oyster-farming there. Arachon oysters have been regarded as a great delicacy since Roman times: they should be consumed on the spot, accompanied by small sausages (crépinettes), eaten piping hot, and dry white wine—Bordeaux, naturally, and preferably Graves.

197 top right Between the Île d'Oléron and the Île d'Aix stands Fort Boyard. Constructed in the middle of the sea in the last century, the strange form of this building has become familiar to the public thanks to numerous films and television programmes.

197 bottom The fort of Chapus, on the other hand, is a more conventional structure. Built in the seventeenth century (it is also known as Fort Louvois), it is located about half a kilometer off the shore near Le Chapus, a small village near Marennes.

198 and 199 *Typical holiday scenes in Brittany: a port where pleasure craft wait for the rising tide to set them afloat again; a large beach where holidaymakers take advantage of the low tide to go horse-riding by the sea.*

200–201 *Off Quiberon,
between Belle-Île and the
mainland, the minute island
of Houat (5 km by 1.3 km or
3 miles by 1 mile) offers day-
trippers the attractions of its
small village and beaches
facing the open sea.*

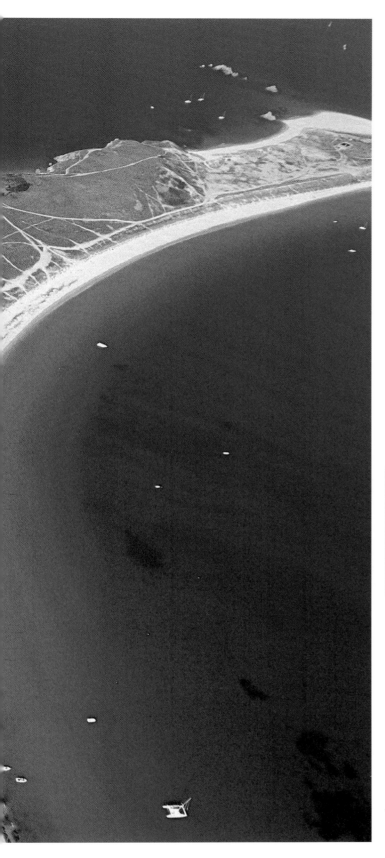

*201 top and bottom
The Bay of Vannes is
part of one of the most
spectacular areas in the
whole of Brittany: the*

*Gulf of Morbihan, a true
inland sea (in Breton,
Mor-bihan means small
sea) dotted with dozens
of tiny islands.*

202 When one looks at Mont-Saint-Michel, it is difficult to know what aspect to focus on: the beauty of its setting, with the immense bay covered by the sea at high tide; the enormous efforts that must have been made to construct this building, from the eleventh to the sixteenth centuries, with all the practical difficulties that had to be faced; the splendor of the monument, described as "one of the wonders of the West," the abbey of which is a masterpiece of Gothic architecture.

203 The archangel Michael stands proudly on the spire of the abbey church at a height of 157 meters (515 feet).

*204 It's odd that there
should be all these
swimming-pools so close to
the clear blue sea.... It's true,
however, that we are at Cap
d'Antibes, a beautiful spot
that seems to invite us to
enjoy the pleasures life has to
offer far from the crowds of
holidaymakers crushed
together on the beaches.*

*205 top Off the coast at
Cannes, the islands of Lérins,
Sainte-Marguerite and Saint-
Honorat permit the visitor to
spend a pleasant day
strolling peacefully in the
shady woods of pines and
eucalyptus—and also,
perhaps, to meditate on the
enigma of the Iron Mask, the
mysterious character
imprisoned by Louis XIV for
many years in the Fort
Royal, on the island of
Sainte-Marguerite, whose
precise identity was never
established.*

*205 bottom The tip of Cap
d'Antibes, between the beach
of Garoupe and the Pointe
de l'Ilette, is the most
wooded part of the
promontory, bordered by a
rocky coast with its warm
colors.*

*206–207 Cap d'Antibes is
one of those places that
seems to have been specially
created for an eternal
holiday. And where could
you hope to find anywhere
better?*

208 and 209 Between Saint-Raphaël and La Napoule, the red rocks of the Estérel blend with the indigo of the Mediterranean in innumerable coves only accessible from the sea.

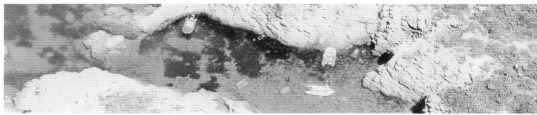

211 bottom Callelongue is certainly one of the most picturesque calanques near Marseilles; a small harbor, a few cottages, an auberge where one can eat in the open air, sipping Bandol rosé or the Côteaux of Aix-en-Provence—doesn't it sound idyllic?

210 Along the coast between Marseilles and Cassis, for over 20 kilometers (12 miles), there is a series of extraordinary piles of rocks, with steep slopes of dazzling white, interspersed here and there by deep inlets—the Calanques, the ideal place for walking and climbing, and also for scuba-diving.

211 top The rugged landscape of the massif of the Calanques. In the upper part of the photograph is Les Goudes, an old fishing village, which is now crowded with Marseillais on Sundays.

212–213 The island of Porquerolles, the most important of the Hyères islands, is largely covered with pine and eucalyptus woods. Having become state property, the island is a nature reserve for the flora of the Mediterranean. Above is the Pointe du Grand Langoustier, the western tip of the island.

213 Scuba-diving and sailing are two of the sports that one can practise at Porquerolles, the small harbor of which, facing the mainland, is seen in the photograph in the center. But one can also go for a walk through the woods, or relax on the wide beaches on the north side of the island.

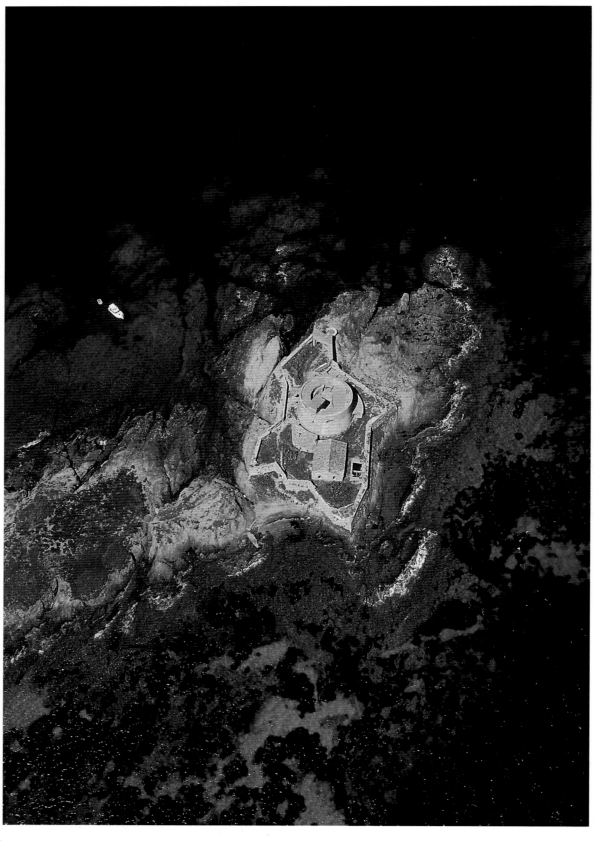

214 The Petit Langoustier, seen here, north of the Pointe du Grand Langoustier, is a rocky islet where there is a small fort, a reminder that in the past Porquerolles was not always as peaceful as it seems to be today.

215 Of the three islands of Lérins, that Île du Levant is now the most unspoilt. Consisting of a long rocky ridge, surrounded by sheer cliffs, it has become a naturist's paradise.

216–217 *South of*
Montpellier, on what was
once a small island and now
forms part of the thin tongue
of land separating the Étang
de Vic from the
Mediterranean, stands the
splendid cathedral of
Maguelone, with its turbulent
past, the massive Romanesque
nave of which continues to
tower above the vineyards.

217 top and bottom
A symphony of different shades of blue in the vast surroundings of Maguelone: étangs and lagoons as far as the eye can see, crossed by the Rhône Canal to Sète and bordered to the south by a narrow coastal strip washed by the deep blue sea of the Gulf of Lions.

218–219 and 220–221
In the Camargue, the production of salt by evaporation dates from antiquity. These are but a few of the salt-pans covering many square miles between Aigues Mortes and the Gulf of Fos-sur-Mer, which at sunset are bathed in a strange reddish light.

*222 and 223 The southern
part of the Camargue is still
a vast barren marshy plain
dotted with étangs and
lagoons that are directly
linked to the sea. This
creates the effect of a lunar
landscape, as may be seen in
this aerial photograph taken
from a high altitude.*

224–225 *In the vast marshy expanses of the south of the Camargue surrounding the Étang de Vaccarès, the fauna is extremely rich, and there are hundreds of species of birds, such as these flamingos seen in flight.*

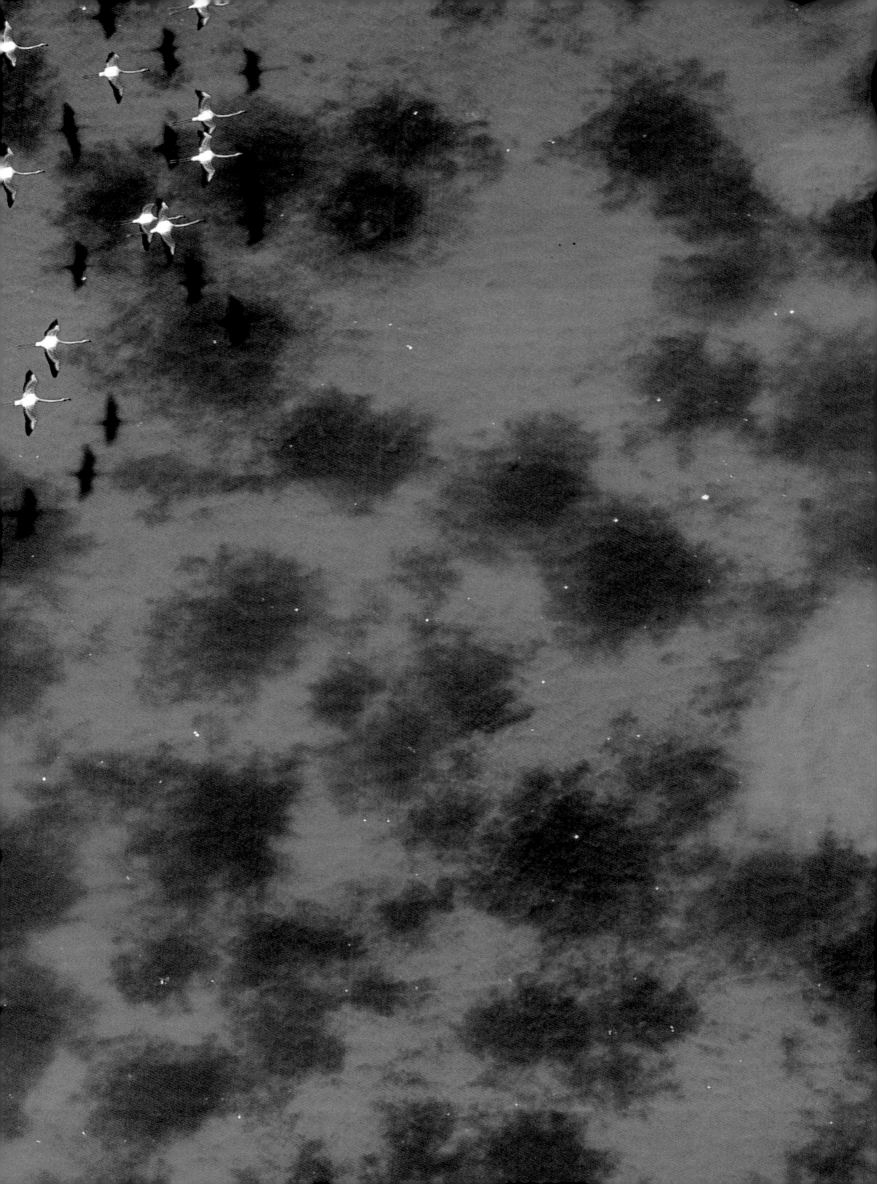

226 top and 226-227
The Grand Rhône, the Petit Rhône, the Vieux Rhône, innumerable pools of brackish water, lagoons separated from the sea by sand-dunes—below Arles, the Rhône splits up into an infinite number of channels that spread out to form a delta recalling, on a smaller scale, the mouths of the great rivers of Asia.

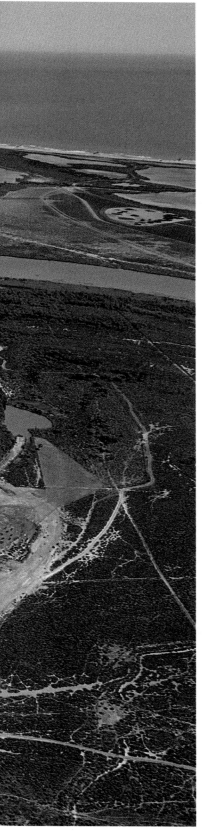

*227 top and 227 bottom
Besides the cultivation of
cereals in the northern part
of the delta, stockbreeding is
one of the main resources of
the Camargue: around the
mas (farms), like the ones
seen here, in the marshy area
of the region there are vast
estates on which the herds of
horses and bulls can wander
freely.*

228 top *East of Paimpol and its bay studded with rocks in northern Brittany, the small lighthouse of Mez du Goëlo stands on a reef completely surrounded by the waves.*

228 center *Fort la Latte is a solid feudal fortress built in the thirteenth and fourteenth centuries to guard the entrance to the Bay of Frénaye. To the west, on the other side of the inlet of Sévignés, Cap Fréhel is well worth a visit, with its high red cliffs against which enormous wave break incessantly, while seagulls and cormorants circle above.*

228 bottom *Off the Côtes d'Armor, the island of Bréhat is surrounded by a multitude of islets and reefs. As is often the case in Brittany, it has a particularly mild climate: mimosa flourishes here and there are even fig-trees and eucalyptus.*

229 *On the west coast of Corsica, the red rocks of what is rightly called Cap Rosso, rise out of the sea with their jagged forms.*

230–231 Off the southern tip of Corsica, near Bonifacio, the small islands of Cavallo and Lavezzi are a paradise for those fond of diving: warm, clear water, a rocky seabed, guaranteed sunshine on the surface–what more could one ask? This is what the celebrities who recently settled on the island of Cavallo must have asked themselves, since the mushrooming of new buildings there has rightly raised the environmentalists' hackles.

232 top and 233 top The sun-drenched west coast of Corsica is extremely indented, with rocky promontories in which there are bays and inlets of all shapes and sizes opening onto the sea with its continually changing colors.

232-233 South of Porto-Vecchio, on the east coast of Corsica, the Bay of Santa Giulia, bordered by a narrow sandy beach, offers a safe haven for passing yachts.

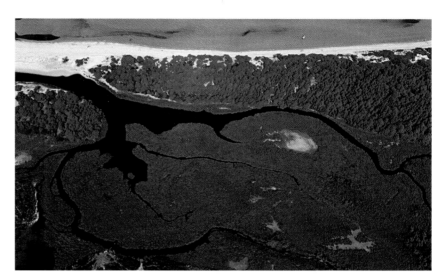

233 bottom On the west coast, in a splendid natural setting with a backdrop of steep mountains, the Gulf of Porto-Vecchio attracts large numbers of tourists from all over the world.

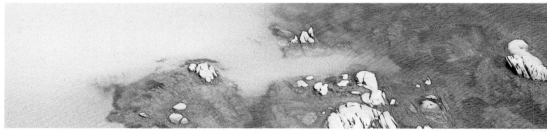

234 and 235 These views
of the east coast of Corsica
speak for themselves: a
solitary sailing boat in the
Bay of Santa Giulia, a
landing stage jutting into
the water sparkling in the
sun, deserted beaches at the
end of an inlet or along
the wooded coast—although
these are everybody's
dreams, it comes as
something of a surprise to
find that in Corsica they
actually correspond to
reality.

236 top and 236-237
Geologically speaking, the area around Bonifacio, on the southern tip of Corsica, with its high, dazzling white limestone cliffs that have been eroded to form strange indentations, is very different from the rest of Corsica, where granite and schist prevail.

236 bottom and 237 top
The high town of Bonifacio, standing on the top of a peninsula flanked by sheer cliffs, is surrounded by the walls built in the sixteenth century by the Genoese, who turned the old city into a virtually impregnable citadel.

238-239 *A view of both the high town of Bonifacio and the low town, on the opposite sides of the narrow harbor mouth. This remarkable location, offering shelter from the sudden Mediterranean storms, was mentioned by Ulysses in the Odyssey.*

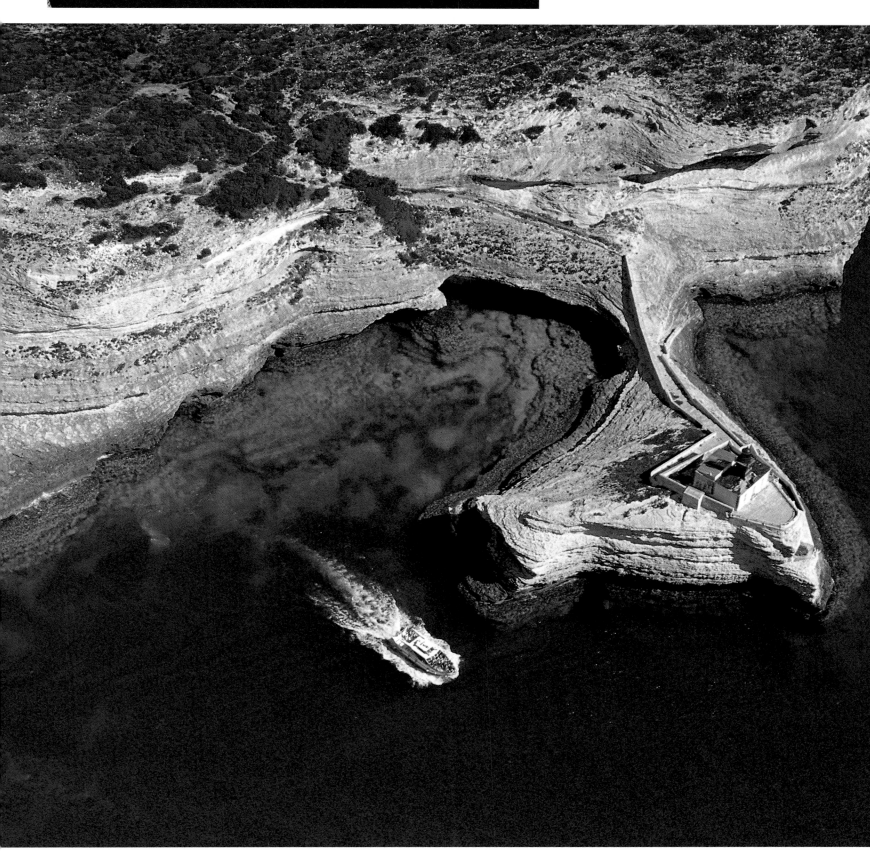

PHOTO CREDITS

All the pictures inside the book are by Guido Alberto Rossi/The Image Bank, except for the following:

Yann Arthus Bertrand/Altitude/The Image Bank: pages 67, 30, 31, 110, 111, 112, 113, 114

Alain Choisnet/The Image Bank: page 145 top

Alain Ernoult/Agence Ernoult Features/The Image Bank: page 64 top

Yannick Le Gal/Agence Ernoult Features/The Image Bank: pages 137, 151 bottom, 228

Alban Lorenzi/Agence Ernoult Features: page 103 top

Daniel Philippe: pages 32-33

Lionel Schwartz/The Image Bank: page 78

Michel Sioux/Agence Ernoult Features/The Image Bank: page 65

Raphaël Van Butsele/Agence Ernoult Features/The Image Bank: pages 79, 103 center

240 The east side of the double ring of fortified walls of Carcassonne, with the tower of Trésau and the two towers with red roofs dominating the Porte Narbonnaise.